Yehya Omeir

Key Stage 2 English Spelling & Vocabulary

WORKBOOK 5

Intermediate Level

Dr Stephen C Curran
with Warren Vokes
Edited by Mark Schofield

This book belongs to

Accelerated Education Publications Ltd

brighter
safest
finer
shining

brightest
cooler
miner
smiling

safer
deeper
hiding
hoping

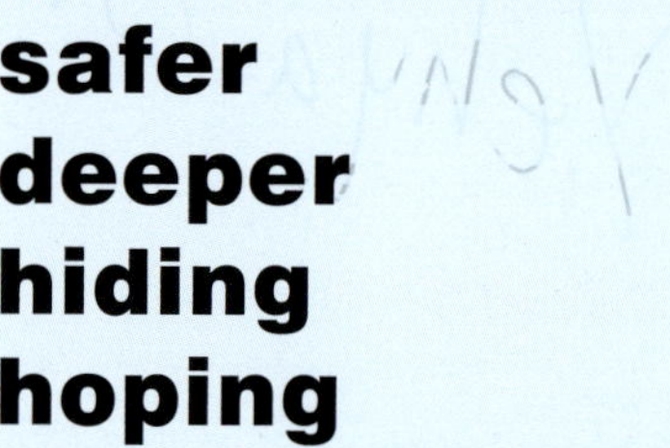

Exercise 93a

1) They were warned not to skate on the frozen lake as the ice was very thin.

2) It is much ______________ to wait behind the motorway barrier if your car breaks down.

3) The ship had come to ______________ on the rocks in the violent storm.

4) The diver descended still ______________ into the dark depths of the sea.

5) The lights went out leaving the room in complete darkness.

6) The __________________ pupils achieved excellent results in the examinations.

7) She could not help ______________ when she thought of the joke he had told her.

8) The ____________ reason for the poor result was his failure to revise.

9) "I was ______________ that you would come and you didn't disappoint me."

10) She discovered the kitten ______________ behind the sofa.

Score /10

Exercise 93b

11) It was a cloudless evening and the moon was ______________ brightly in the night sky.

12) "We're all going ________________ at the local ice rink. Would you like to come too?"

13) The rain clouds had passed over and the sky was looking much __________________ .

14) Caster sugar is much ____________ than granulated sugar.

15) He suffered from a very serious ____________ but now he is fully recovered.

16) The ______________ way to cross a busy road is to use the pelican crossing.

17) It was a very hot day but much ______________ in the shade under the tree.

18) She had seen the ___________ steal the handbag and gave a statement to the police.

19) His father had been a miner and now he too worked down the pit.

20) Their skin had been ______________ by the sun's ultra violet rays.

Score /10

skate	**skating**
darkness	**illness**
chief	**thief**
grief	**burnt**

Word Bank TOTAL 1,860

Across

93

1. Giving out light.
4. Bottom-dwelling marine fish with a flattened body.
7. Somebody who steals.
8. Giving off stronger light.
10. A disease or sickness.
13. The absence of light.
15. Lower in pitch.
16. The person with the most authority in a group.
17. Great sadness.
18. Least likely to cause harm.

Put the mystery letter (✱) into the box marked **93** below. Add in the mystery letters from puzzles **94** to **100** then rearrange them to make **Dickens's Mystery Word**.

The clue is **TREE**.

Down

2. Wishing something to be true.
3. Sliding along a slippery surface.
5. Less coarse.
6. Reflecting the strongest light.
8. Destroyed by fire.
9. Concealing from view.
11. Making a pleasant expression.
12. Someone who digs underground for coal.
14. Less likely to result in injury or damage.
16. Colder, but usually pleasantly so.

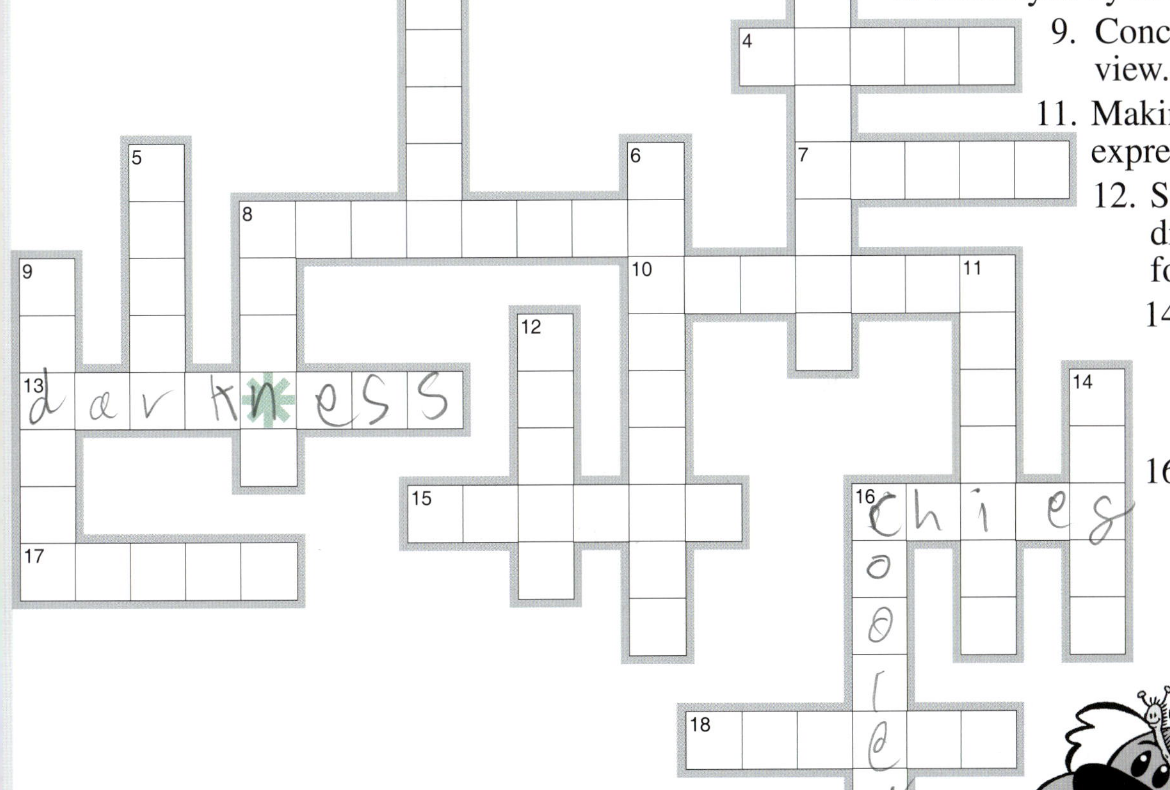

	93	94	95	96	97	98	99	100
Enter your mystery letters here:								

Now rearrange them:

Mystery Word:

Score

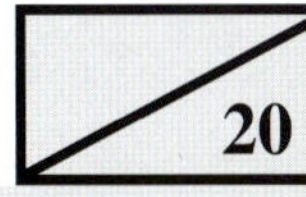

should	**cheer**	**quickly**
nearly	**write**	**writing**
wrote	**wrap**	**prove**
move	**remove**	**repeat**

Across

94

1. Words written down.
5. Modelling substance.
7. To coil around something.
10. Christian festival commemorating the resurrection of Jesus Christ.
12. To change position.
13. Almost but not quite.
15. Somebody who writes poems.
18. To make a casual comment or observation.
19. To take away something.

Down

2. Fix or mend something.
3. Having the colour of ash or lead.
4. Christian festival celebrating the birth of Jesus Christ.
6. Moving or doing something fast.
7. Composed and sent a letter.
8. A piece written in verse.
9. Establish the truth or existence of something.
11. To be scheduled or expected to be.
14. Say something again.
16. Put words on paper.
17. Shout of approval.

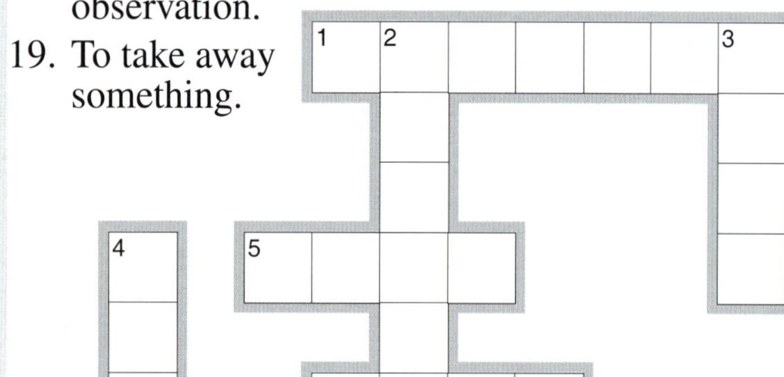

Mystery Letter

Score

/20

grey	**clay**	**Word Bank TOTAL 1,880**
poem	**poet**	
remark	**repair**	
Easter	**Christmas**	

Exercise 94a

1) At ______________ we were given lots of chocolate eggs.

2) William Wordsworth, the famous English ___________ , wrote *The Daffodils*.

3) John ____________ home to his parents every week while away at boarding school.

4) She was rushing in the heavy traffic and ____________ had an accident.

5) "I will say the phrase once, then you _____________ it after me."

6) The potter threw another lump of ___________ onto the wheel and began again.

7) If you wish to stay healthy you ___________ take lots of exercise.

8) I asked the jeweller if he could ___________ the broken clasp on my bracelet.

9) I always attend midnight Mass on _________________ Eve.

10) She managed to ______________ the splinter from his finger.

Score /10

Exercise 94b

11) She recited the ___________ which she had written especially for the occasion.

12) "Come _____________ , they are showing the rocket launch on television right now."

13) The ability to read and ___________ are two basic skills that everyone should learn.

14) They suspected he was guilty but they could not __________ it.

15) It was only a casual, off-the-cuff _____________ but it caused great offence.

16) J. K. Rowling is famous the world over for ____________ the *Harry Potter* books.

17) When he won, a huge __________ from his supporters echoed round the stadium.

18) He found some pretty paper with which to ___________ her birthday present.

19) For his interview he wore a neutral-coloured dark ___________ suit.

20) "It's your turn: shake the dice and ___________ your counter."

Score /10

aloud
afraid
cloak
afternoon
around
coal
float
however
alike
roast
yesterday
breakfast

Exercise 95a

1) She was a ______________________ now that her daughter had given birth to a son.

2) Every morning he ate _________________ before going to school.

3) A new ______________ of his favourite bookshop opened in the town.

4) Today is Tuesday, so the day before __________________ was Sunday.

5) "We need some more __________ for the fire: could you refill the scuttle?"

6) I ordered a fruit sundae and my mum had a ____________ Melba.

7) It's not often you see a ___________ chestnut vendor on the street.

8) He turned the car _____________ and headed back the way he had come.

9) Although he sometimes took the bus, it was more ___________ for him to cycle.

10) "We thought we'd lost you. _____________ did you find us?"

Score / **10**

Exercise 95b

11) In the storm several ________________ had been ripped from the trees.

12) "Meet me for lunch at one o'clock tomorrow __________________ ."

13) He increased the length of line beneath the ___________ to fish nearer to the bottom.

14) "I'm _____________ she won't be in today - can I take a message?"

15) Cattle and wild ponies are allowed to ___________ throughout the New Forest.

16) She stood in front of the class and read ___________ a passage from the book.

17) He could just hear their shouts __________ the roar of the water rushing past.

18) He opened a tin of _______________ , drained off the syrup and put them in a dish.

19) She threw her ___________ over her shoulders and fastened the frog.

20) The twins were so ___________ they were almost identical.

Score / **10**

roam	**grandmother**
above	**usual**
branch	**branches**
peach	**peaches**

Word Bank TOTAL 1,900

95

Across

1. Part of a tree growing from the trunk.
4. Normal, customary or typical.
5. On all sides of or somewhere near.
7. A loose, sleeveless outer garment.
9. Sweet, round, juicy fruits with a stone.
12. The mother of your father or mother.
15. Rest on the surface of a liquid.
16. Frightened.
17. First meal of the day.
19. Local units of an organisation.
20. The day before this one.

Down

2. Using an audible speaking voice.
3. In whatever way or to whatever degree.
6. Creamy orange colour tinged with yellow.
8. Similar in appearance.
10. Daytime between noon and evening.
11. Black rock used as fuel.
13. Directly overhead.
14. To wander aimlessly.
18. Oven-cooked meat.

Mystery Letter

Score /20

classes	**glasses**	**order**
border	**together**	**towards**
afterwards	**forward**	**inches**
worth	**starve**	**husband**

96

Across

2. A woman's spouse.
8. In company with others in a group.
12. Weaken or die through hunger.
13. In a particular direction.
14. A hot condiment.
15. Fill by pushing things into it.
17. Periods of teaching.
18. At a later time than that mentioned previously.

Down

1. Moves by small degrees.
3. Two times.
4. Towards the front.
5. Instruction to do something.
6. Outer eyewear.
7. Subsequently or because.
9. A band running along the edge.
10. Large pot used to boil water.
11. Something's monetary value.
14. Cost of something bought or sold.
16. Enclosing structure usually made of wood.
17. End of the sleeve nearest the wrist.

price
since
pepper
cuff
twice
fence
copper
stuff

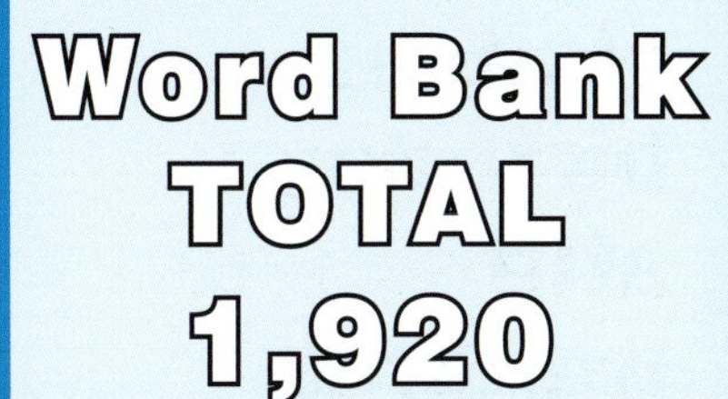

Exercise 96a

1) All she had to do then was to ____________ the turkey and wrap it in cooking foil.

2) There were three ______________ : one for white wine; one for red; and one for water.

3) The bride and her new _______________ posed with their families for photographs.

4) They checked the compass bearing and set off ______________ the far hill.

5) "If you all move _______________ a little, we can get more people in behind you."

6) They travelled south through Texas and crossed the ____________ into Mexico.

7) The torch flashed ____________ and then once again. Three flashes, that was the signal.

8) Last weekend my dad and our neighbour replaced the garden ______________ .

9) As he went to shake my hand, I noticed that his shirt _________ was frayed.

10) ______________ is an excellent conductor of electricity and heat.

Score ___ / 10

Exercise 96b

11) The car collection at Beaulieu must be ____________ millions of pounds.

12) They walked ___________________ , hand in hand, along the towpath.

13) They saw the show and ___________________ had a meal in a nearby restaurant.

14) Dancing ______________ were held in the church hall and Lucy wanted to enrol.

15) The two cars narrowly avoided a collision and missed by only a few ___________ .

16) He never used the salt from the cruet but he liked lots of pepper .

17) The crops have failed due to the drought and many people could ______________ .

18) We were at school together but we have not seen each other ___________ then.

19) In the library all the books are in alphabetical ____________ by author.

20) "I bought it in the sale at a greatly reduced _____________ ."

Score ___ / 10

visit	**fir**	**birth**
birthday	**bitter**	**silly**
stiff	**hurry**	**provide**
pretend	**forest**	**track**

Exercise 97a

1) It was so ____________ that you could hear a pin drop.

2) They sent out many cards to announce the ______________ of their second child.

3) The menu in the Chinese restaurant listed a huge variety of _______________ .

4) He asked the manufacturer to ______________ a list of spare parts.

5) Following the narrow _____________ through the woods, they came to a clearing.

6) The dense ____________ of conifer trees was being grown for paper production.

7) He asked his closest ____________ to be the best man at his wedding.

8) When they were all ______________ the instructor began the training.

9) She was driving so she ordered a non-alcoholic drink of bitter lemon.

10) A collection of ______ cones was on display on the nature table.

Score /10

Exercise 97b

11) It is her thirteenth ________________ and she is now a teenager.

12) The overnight frost had frozen the washing on the line and made it ___________ .

13) The little boy would _______________ he had a playmate when he played on his own.

14) A slice of _____________ is often added to tea instead of milk or sugar.

15) Simon had a sweet tooth and covered his cereal with far too much ____________ .

16) When her father was in hospital, Victoria would __________ him every evening.

17) His job was to make up and fill the ____________ , then seal the lids with vinyl tape.

18) The old document showed that his family used to ___________ in the little cottage.

19) It was a ____________ thing to have done and now he felt very foolish.

20) " _____________ up, we're going to miss the train!"

Score /10

dwell
lemon
friend
boxes
present
sugar
quiet
dishes

Word Bank TOTAL 1,940

Across

97

6. Making little or no noise.
7. In a particular place.
8. Somebody emotionally close to another.
11. Make available.
12. Evergreen tree with needle-shaped leaves.
14. Containers for serving food.
15. Ridiculous.
17. Event of being born.
18. Mark left by a moving person, animal or thing.

Down

1. Fights using fists.
2. Day somebody is born.
3. Go to see someone.
4. White or brown sweet-tasting substance.
5. Rigid, inflexible or hard to move.
8. Large dense growth of trees.
9. Reside.
10. Rush or speed up.
11. To make believe.
13. Strong and sharp in taste.
16. Yellow or green citrus fruit.

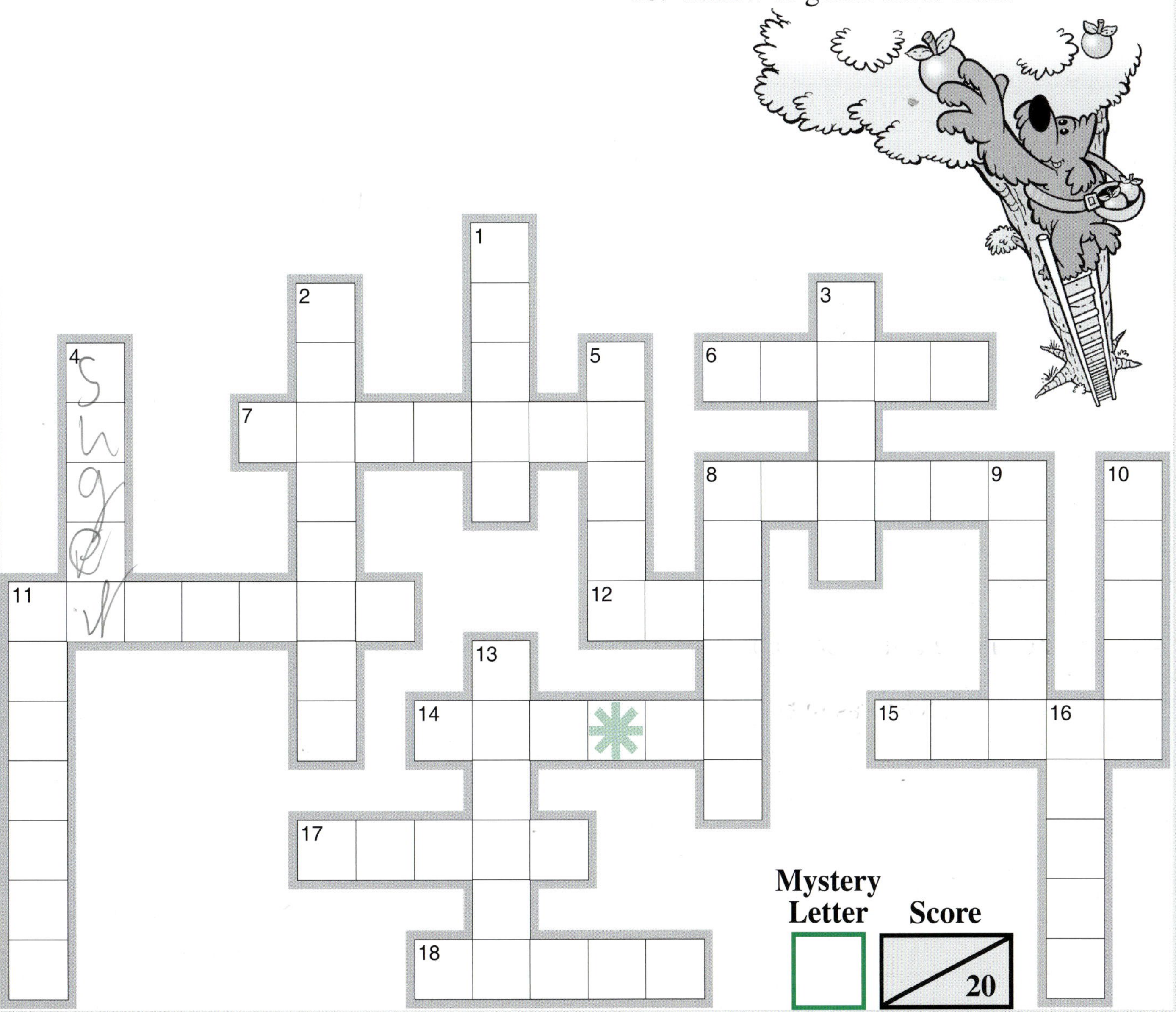

finger	**flesh**	**wool**
bloom	**cling**	**strip**
pint	**gift**	**serve**
person	**term**	**upset**

Across

98

3. Hold tightly with hands or arms.
5. An individual human being.
7. Sheep's short curly hair.
10. Team of 11 players, for example a football, hockey or cricket team.
12. A bouncing cricket shot to the boundary.
13. Soft tissue of the body.
15. Overturned or spilled.
16. A musical interval equal to an octave plus a third.
18. Digit of the hand.
19. A special talent or skill that someone appears to be have been born with.

Down

1. To open into flower.
2. Easy to do, understand or work out.
4. To put a ball or shuttlecock in play.
6. The number 12.
8. Division of an academic year.
9. Remove old paint or varnish.
11. Item number five in a series.
12. One of four equal parts.
14. The digit three places to the left of the decimal point.
17. Unit of liquid measurement.

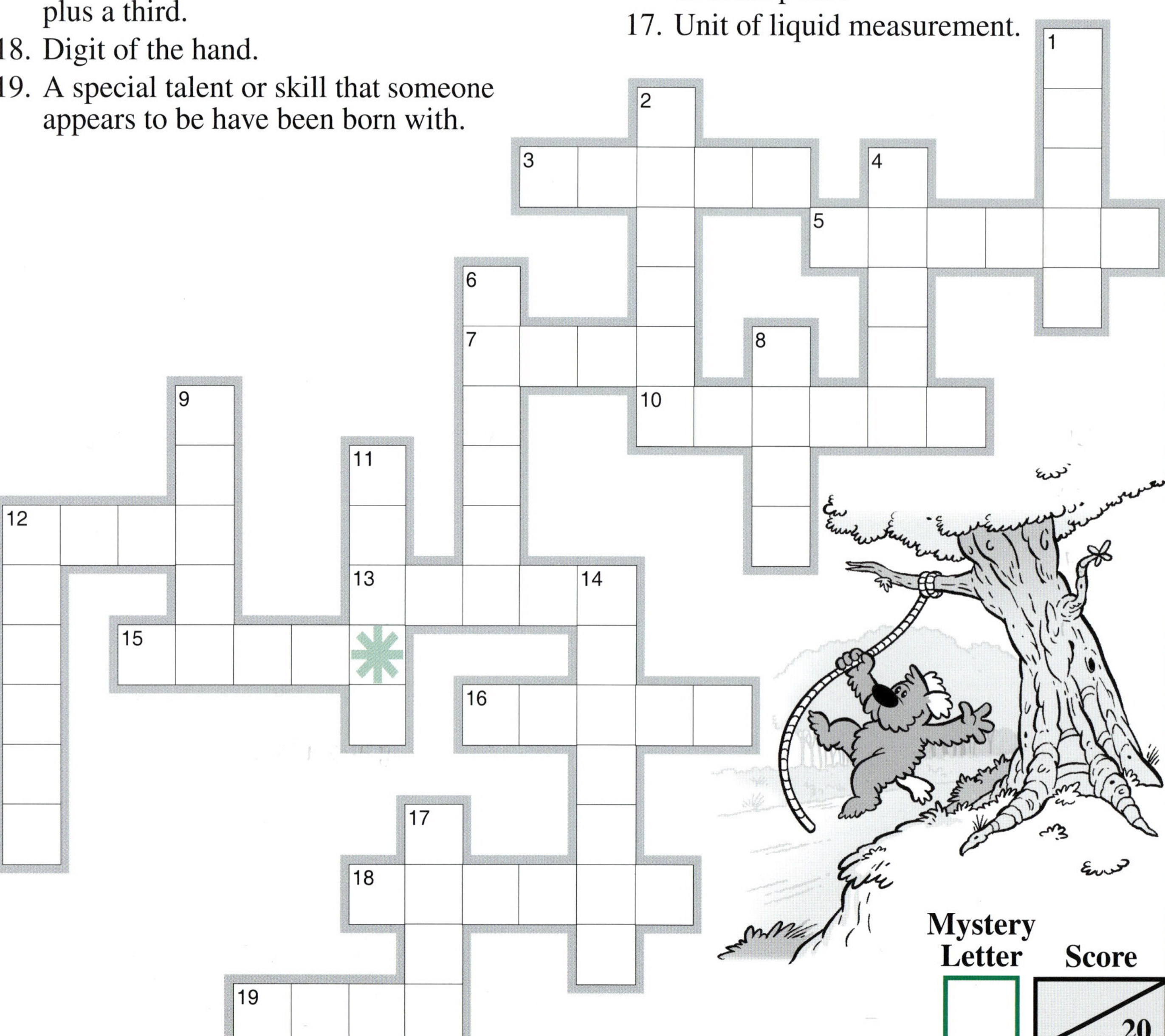

four
fifth
eleven
twelve
fourth
tenth
simple
hundred

Word Bank TOTAL 1,960

Exercise 98a

1) The United States celebrates Independence Day on the ____________ of July.

2) The football team only had ten players and needed one more to make ____________ .

3) The runway at Nice airport is just a ____________ of land built offshore.

4) The instructions were ______________ and easy to follow.

5) His new shoes were rubbing, so he put some sheep's _________ inside his sock.

6) His first four shots failed to hit the target but his __________ was a bull's eye.

7) The ____________ was an ace and unplayable by her opponent.

8) There are one ______________ cents in one Euro.

9) She was very ___________ and her friend tried to console her.

10) He could not remember the ___________ and final commandment.

Score /10

Exercise 98b

11) It was the end of the school __________ and now they had three weeks' holiday.

12) The small child was still afraid and continued to ___________ tightly to his mother.

13) He cut his ____________ opening the tin and needed a plaster to stop the bleeding.

14) The dog had not eaten for days and had little _____________ on his bones.

15) It was her last day at the firm and her workmates bought her a small _________ .

16) Christine put the custard powder into the __________ jug and added boiling water.

17) "The ____________ who did this has upset the whole class and should be ashamed."

18) A square, rectangle, trapezium, rhombus and rhomboid all have _________ sides.

19) The flowers at the horticultural show were all in full ____________ .

20) The _____________ disciples joined Jesus for the Last Supper.

Score /10

daisy	daisies	lily
lilies	wise	spider
soap	soak	earn
earth	grace	space

Exercise 99a

1) Climbing the ____________ slope was difficult, especially carrying heavy rucksacks.

2) He ran out of ____________ and could not fit any more CDs into the rack.

3) After exercising, she liked to ____________ in a hot bath for fifteen minutes.

4) He watched the ______________ spinning its web and was fascinated by the process.

5) He had a puncture and had to change the ______________ at the roadside.

6) The drought had lasted many weeks and the ____________ was dry and cracked.

7) A frog sat on the large, flat leaf of a water __________ .

8) Although he was very tired and sore, he ran on _______________ and finished the race.

9) She was not sure but she took a ______________ and guessed the answer correctly.

10) It was a very brave ____________ and he was awarded a medal.

Score /10

Exercise 99b

11) The padlock was made from hardened ___________ and was extremely strong.

12) Sean had a clear soprano ____________ and sang in the school choir.

13) Anna worked on Saturdays to _____________ some extra pocket money.

14) The old man had lived a full and varied life and was very ______________ .

15) She planned to ____________ all her friends to her summer barbecue.

16) She taught her young son to wash his hands with ___________ and hot water.

17) "Sit here on the grass and I'll show you all how to make a _____________ chain."

18) They picked the ______________ and strung them together by slitting their stems.

19) On top of the coffin was a wreath of white _____________ from his wife.

20) He asked the minister to say _____________ before the meal.

Score /10

voice
invite
steep
wheel

bravely
chance
steel
deed

Word Bank TOTAL 1,980

Across

99

2. To move quickly in a circle.
4. Plant with short stems and flowers with white or pinkish-white petals.
6. Cleansing agent.
11. Soft, workable material in which plants grow.
13. Sound made by using vocal organs.
14. Make money by working.
15. Strong alloy of iron and carbon.
16. Knowing much from experience.
17. Make something or somebody completely wet.
18. A prayer at mealtimes.

Down

1. An intentional act.
3. Perennial plant that has layered bulbs, blade-shaped leaves and single large flowers.

Down (continued)

5. To set things some distance apart.
6. An arachnid that spins webs.
7. Plural of *3 Down*.
8. The likelihood that something will happen.
9. Acting in a manner showing courage when faced with danger, difficulty or pain.
10. To ask to participate.
12. Tall plants that have flowers with white petals radiating from a round yellow centre.
15. To soak something in a liquid, especially for cleaning or softening or to extract something.

Mystery Letter

Score /20

thirteen	**fourteen**	**fifteen**
sixteen	**thirty**	**twenty**
fifty	**sixty**	**thousand**
creeping	**indeed**	**between**

Exercise 100a

1) The ____________ Years' War was fought in Europe between 1618 and 1648.

2) Four score (four times ______________) equals eighty.

3) Jesus fed the five _________________ with five loaves and two fishes.

4) He broke the ______________ and distributed them among those present.

5) Only a few metres remained _______________ him and the winning post.

6) She divided the chewy bar into two equal _____________ and gave the boys one each.

7) The _____________ made off on foot with the stolen goods.

8) He arrived at eight forty-five: ____________ minutes before the nine o'clock meeting.

9) The tide was coming in and the sea was ________________ slowly up the beach.

10) She retired at the age of ___________ and drew her pension.

Score / 10

Exercise 100b

11) Many superstitious people consider the number ________________ to be unlucky.

12) At _______________ she was old enough to learn to ride a motor scooter.

13) "Would you prefer a brown __________ or a white one?"

14) The new-born ___________ was suckling milk from its mother's udder.

15) It cost £48.50. He paid with a ___________ pound note and received £1.50 in change.

16) The ___________ was too high for her to reach, so she fetched some steps.

17) She had eaten six of the twenty sweets and now there were only _______________ left.

18) "He's not a very good eater and often ______________ half his meal untouched."

19) "I expect the __________ he does eat is enough for him."

20) He was very keen, ______________ eager, to have a go himself.

Score / 10

half	**calf**
shelf	**loaf**
halves	**leaves**
thieves	**loaves**

Word Bank TOTAL 2,000

Across

100

2. Fourth digit to the left of the decimal point.
5. Group of 14 objects.
6. Young cow or bull.
14. Steals.
15. A score of things.
16. Number 50.
17. From one place to another.
18. Number 13.

Down

1. What is more.
3. Number 60.
4. Spend time lazily.
5. A team of 15 players, especially a rugby union team.
6. Developing or advancing gradually over a period of time.
7. Quantities of bread shaped and baked as a whole.

Down (continued)

8. Score in tennis awarded to the player with a score of fifteen on winning another point.
9. A ledge of rock, sand, or ice.
10. Something with a value of 16.
11. Hinged or removable sections of a table top.
12. Two equal periods of play into which some games are divided.
13. One of two equal parts.

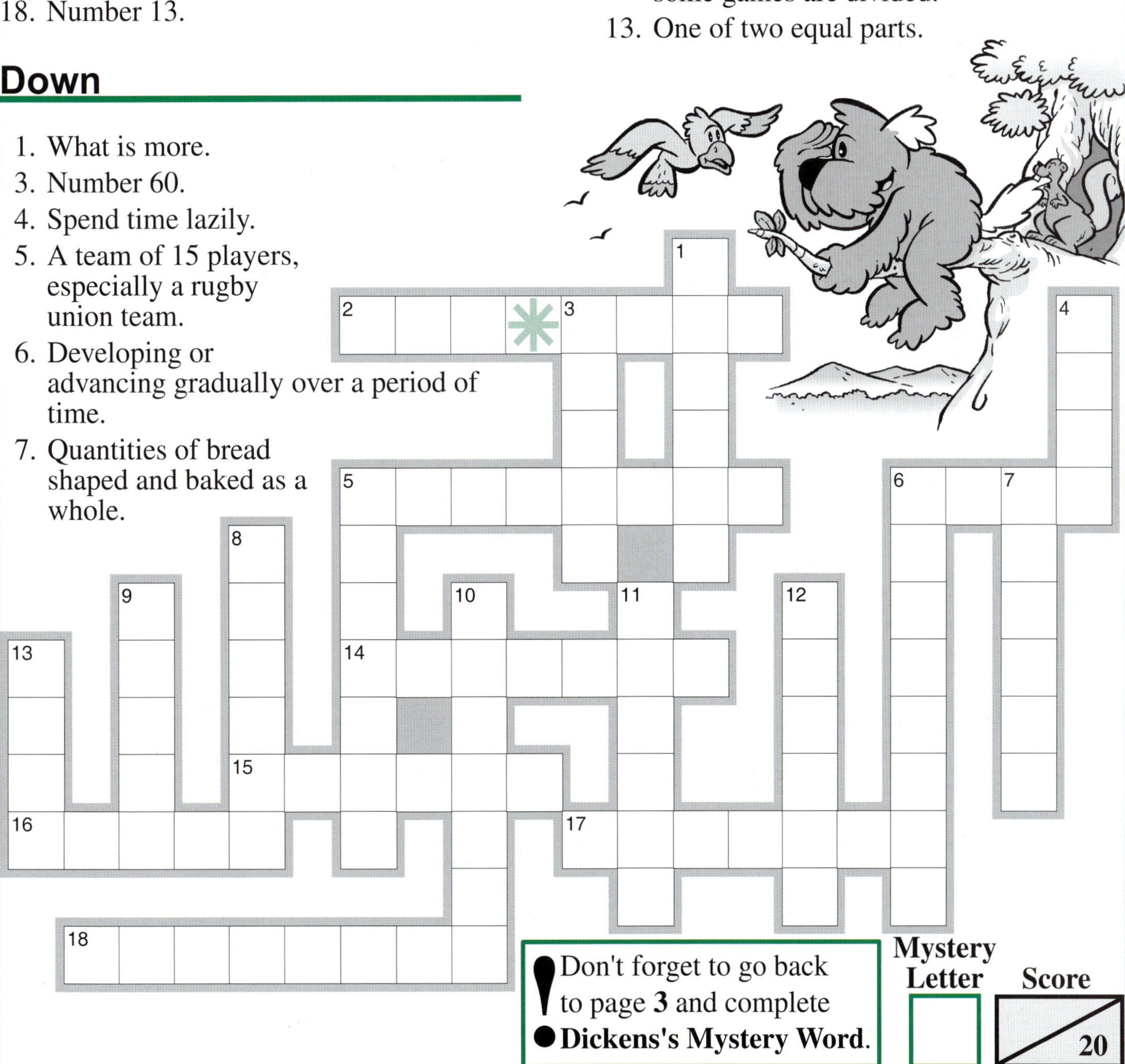

Don't forget to go back to page **3** and complete **Dickens's Mystery Word**.

Mystery Letter

Score 20

In the Living Room

Can you find all these words in the picture below? Write the correct word against each number.

settee	**armchair**	**vase**	**newspaper**	**television**
bookcase	**mantelpiece**	**plant**	**plug**	**speaker**
cushion	**magazine**	**hearth**	**pen**	**candle**

1.______________________ 2.______________________ 3.______________________

4.______________________ 5.______________________ 6.______________________

7.______________________ 8.______________________ 9.______________________

10.______________________ 11.______________________ 12.______________________

13.______________________ 14.______________________ 15.______________________

In the Bathroom

Can you find all these words in the picture below? Write the correct word against each number. When you have finished you can colour in the picture if you want to.

scales	**wash basin**	**shower**	**toothpaste**	**razor**
cistern	**toothbrush**	**water**	**taps**	**pedestal**
shower gel	**mat**	**towel**	**toilet**	**soap**

1.______________________ 2.______________________ 3.______________________

4.______________________ 5.______________________ 6.______________________

7.______________________ 8.______________________ 9.______________________

10.______________________ 11.______________________ 12.______________________

13.______________________ 14.______________________ 15.______________________

flew	**threw**	**crew**
chew	**wolf**	**themselves**
grind	**thrown**	**knee**
kneel	**knot**	**knock**

Exercise 101a

1) He could escape if he could just manage to untie the ____________ in the rope.

2) It was an error of judgement and they had only ___________________ to blame.

3) He had asked the builder to repair it but still it had not been __________ .

4) The aircraft refuelled at Singapore and then ___________ on to Australia.

5) Her horse stopped abruptly at the hurdle and she was _____________ from the saddle.

6) She sent off for a new set of kitchen _____________ that she saw in an advertisement.

7) The _crew_ of the *Enola Gay* dropped the atom bomb on Hiroshima.

8) He would always ___________ his food thoroughly to help his digestion.

9) "Don't __________ down your food, you'll get indigestion!"

10) He was kept in ________ overnight and questioned next morning.

Score /10

Exercise 101b

11) The old man's progress along the corridor was __________ - paced and painfully slow.

12) While the men went to watch the game, their _______________ went shopping.

13) "I put it in the __________ last week, so it should have been delivered by now."

14) The bell seemed not to be working, so he gave a loud _____________ on the door.

15) "Would the boys at the very front ____________ down for the photograph."

16) He had an operation on his ___________ to repair the patella.

17) He _____________ the ball in from the boundary and the wicket-keeper caught it.

18) The _________ was broken and the express train left the track at high speed.

19) My dad uses an electric carving _____________ for the roast joint on Sunday.

20) Her husband would ___________ his teeth while he slept.

Score /10

knife	**knives**
wives	**fixed**
mail	**rail**
snail	**jail**

Word Bank TOTAL 2,020

101

Across

1. Tool for cutting or spreading.
4. To hit repeatedly.
5. To pulverise something.
6. Past participle of *'throw'*.
7. Plural of *'wife'*.
10. Their normal selves.
12. Place where criminals are kept.
13. Securely in position.
15. Travelled on an aircraft.
16. Long length of wood or metal to hang things from.
17. Gnaw something repeatedly.

Down

1. Way of tying a length of rope, string, thread, or other material.
2. Tools with a sharp blade and a handle.
3. To rest on, or get down on, one or both knees.
4. Middle joint of the human leg.
8. Gastropod with a coiled shell and a retractable muscular foot.
9. Carnivore that hunts in packs.
10. Past tense of *'throw'*.
11. Items sent in a postal system.
14. Ship's staff excluding officers.

Put the mystery letters from the starred squares (✱) from puzzles **101** to **107** into their numbered box below, then rearrange them to make **Kate's Mystery Word**. The clue is **FRUIT**.

Enter your mystery letters:

101	102	103	104	105	106	107

Now rearrange them to make the:

Mystery Word:

flock
tied
trunk
sure
finish
raise
strike
pure
tie
raised
cure
picture

Across

102

2. Take somebody prisoner.
6. Group of birds or sheep.
10. Perfect dwelling place after death.
11. Unquestioningly true or real.
12. On the point of death.
13. To restore a sick animal or person to health.
15. To feel extremely frightened or worried about something that may happen in the future.
17. To come to, or bring something to an end.
18. Not mixed with any other substance.
19. Completely or partially unable to hear in one or both ears.
20. Given money in return for work.

Down

1. An equal score or result in a game, race or competition.
3. Something drawn or painted.
4. To act as a parent or guardian to somebody while he or she is growing up.
5. Large travelling case.
7. Deliberately saying something untrue.
8. Made a knot.
9. Moved something to a higher level.
14. To stop working as a protest.
16. Protect somebody or something from attack, harm, or danger.

Mystery Letter

Score

20

capture	**defend**
dying	**lying**
dread	**deaf**
heaven	**paid**

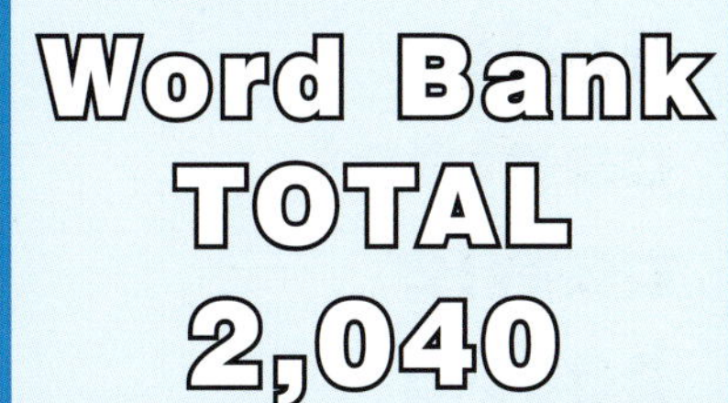

Exercise 102a

1) The animal was very sick and was clearly ____________ of the disease.

2) He saw the older boy ____________ the younger one, who then fell to the ground.

3) She showed her art teacher the _______________ that she had painted.

4) He was profoundly ___________ in both ears and had not heard the bus approaching.

5) Teams of experts finally managed to _____________ the *Mary Rose* from the sea bed.

6) "You have five minutes left to _____________ the test."

7) He __________ his entrance money at the kiosk and went into the exhibition.

8) He thought he would be able to do it easily but now he was not so ___________ .

9) They all stood and ______________ their glasses for the loyal toast.

10) The condition was terminal with no known ________ .

Score /10

Exercise 102b

11) "This place would be ______________ , if it weren't for the people that live here!"

12) They managed to _______________ two enemy soldiers for interrogation.

13) The elephant extended its ____________ towards them and sniffed loudly.

14) She used to _____________ Mondays because the first lesson was double maths.

15) "I know you are ____________ , Tomkins. Tell me the truth and I will not punish you."

16) The shepherd tended his ___________ of sheep and brought them down from the hills.

17) He bent down to ________ his shoelace and the man behind walked into him.

18) The spring water was clear and tasted very __________ .

19) The soldiers tried to _____________ their position but they were overrun.

20) The match was ___________ with three goals each.

Score /10

built	**build**	**building**
content	**battle**	**rattle**
cattle	**tired**	**kettle**
bottle	**cork**	**sore**

Exercise 103a

1) "Put the ____________ on and we'll have a nice cup of tea."

2) We watched the dolphins ___________________ ahead of the ship's bow.

3) Trafalgar was a very intense naval ____________ with many casualties on both sides.

4) The critics did not __________ the film very highly but I enjoyed it immensely.

5) He was very arrogant and his _______________ was very condescending.

6) "The castle's haunted and sometimes you can hear the ____________ of chains."

7) He __________ the house himself and it took him nearly four years to complete.

8) She took the painting to an art gallery and asked them to ____________ it for her.

9) No ______________ how hard she tried, she could not follow the knitting pattern.

10) He slowed the car down to cross the _____________ grid.

Score ___ / 10

Exercise 103b

11) He used a penknife to ______________ the dried mud off his shoes.

12) The milkman had dropped a ___________ and there was milk all over the pavement.

13) The roof and windows of the old _______________ needed much restoration.

14) Never _______________ to leave work for others, she always offered to help.

15) Coming down the wet stairs too quickly, she ______________ and sprained her ankle.

16) His skin was very __________ with sunburn and the bedcovers aggravated the pain.

17) The Olympic ___________ was carried across the country by a series of runners.

18) He pulled the __________ from the bottle and poured them both a glass of wine.

19) She was so _____________ she could hardly keep her eyes open.

20) It was a close match and the tension began to ___________ .

Score ___ / 10

rate
frame
swimming
matter
flame
scrape
slipped
manner

Word Bank TOTAL 2,060

103

Across

7. Quite satisfied and happy.
8. To move something hard, sharp, or rough across a surface.
9. A surrounding structure.
10. To set a value on something.
11. Cylindrical piece of material used as a bottle stopper.
13. Made a structure by fitting the parts of it together.
14. A structure with walls and a roof.
15. Slid out of the proper or desired position.
16. Container for boiling water.
17. A painful open skin infection or wound.

Down

1. To preserve fruit or vegetables in a glass container.
2. The way in which something is done or happens.
3. Needing rest.
4. A substance or material of a particular kind.
5. Moving unsupported through the water using the arms and legs.
6. Hot glowing body of burning gas.
10. To make somebody lose his or her composure.
11. Farm animals of the ox family.
12. The physical structure, shape and size of a person.
13. A large-scale fight between armed forces.

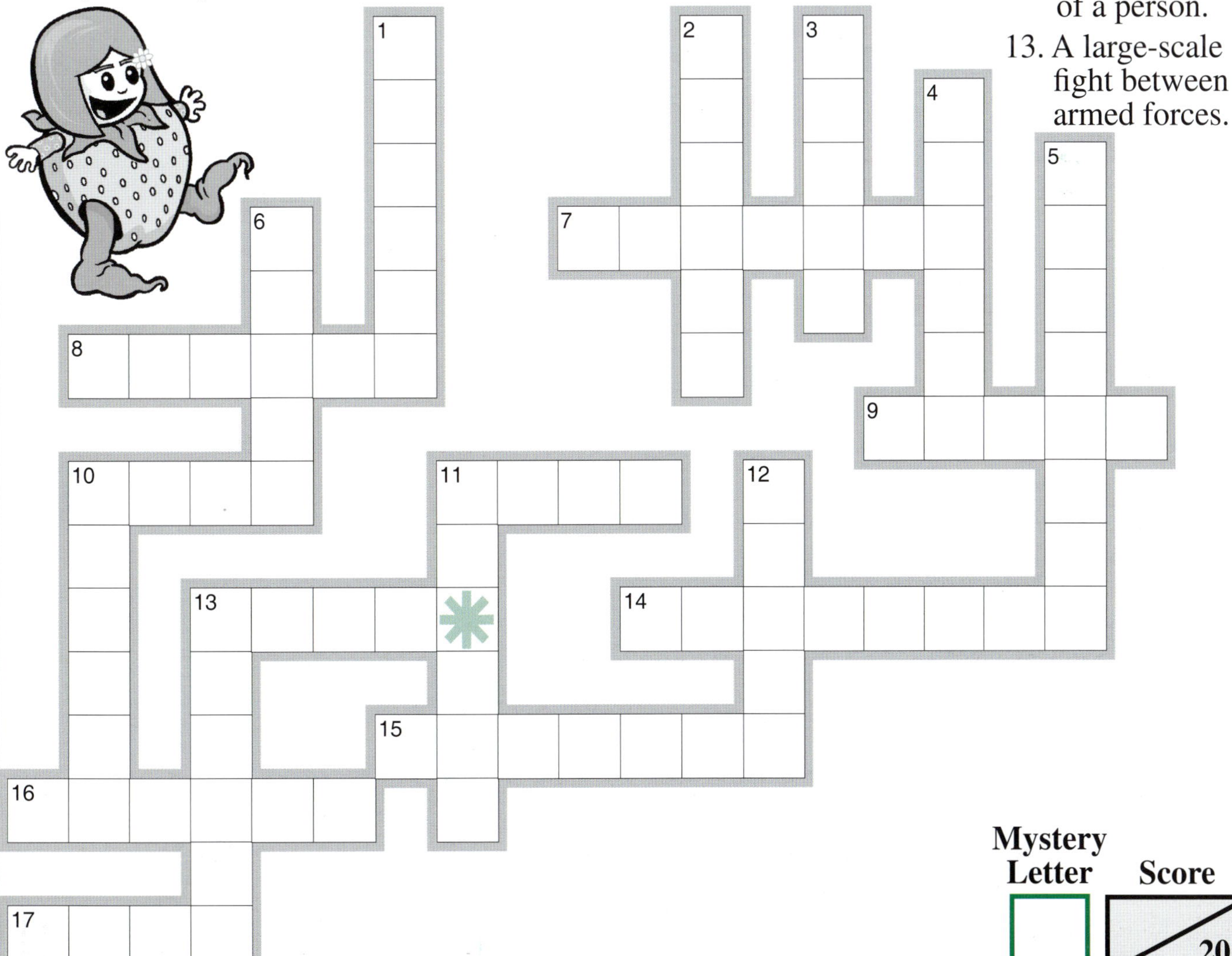

Mystery Letter

Score
20

toe
axe
army
spy
scout
trying
rank
butterflies
shout
flying
shy
answer

Across

104

2. Large armed fighting force.
5. Without difficulty or strain.
6. To engage in espionage.
7. Utter something very loudly.
10. High status.
11. Armed conflict between countries.
13. A digit of the foot.
14. Response to a question.
15. Uncomfortable in the company of others.
19. Even less difficult.
20. Insects with two pairs of brightly coloured wings.

Down

1. Lively and cheerfully.
3. Happening or passing very quickly.
4. The superlative of '*easy*'.
8. Weighing the most.
9. Placing great strain on somebody's patience, composure, or good nature.
12. Weighing a lot.
16. Weighing even more.
17. To cut something, for example expenditures or services, drastically.
18. To gather information about an enemy's position.

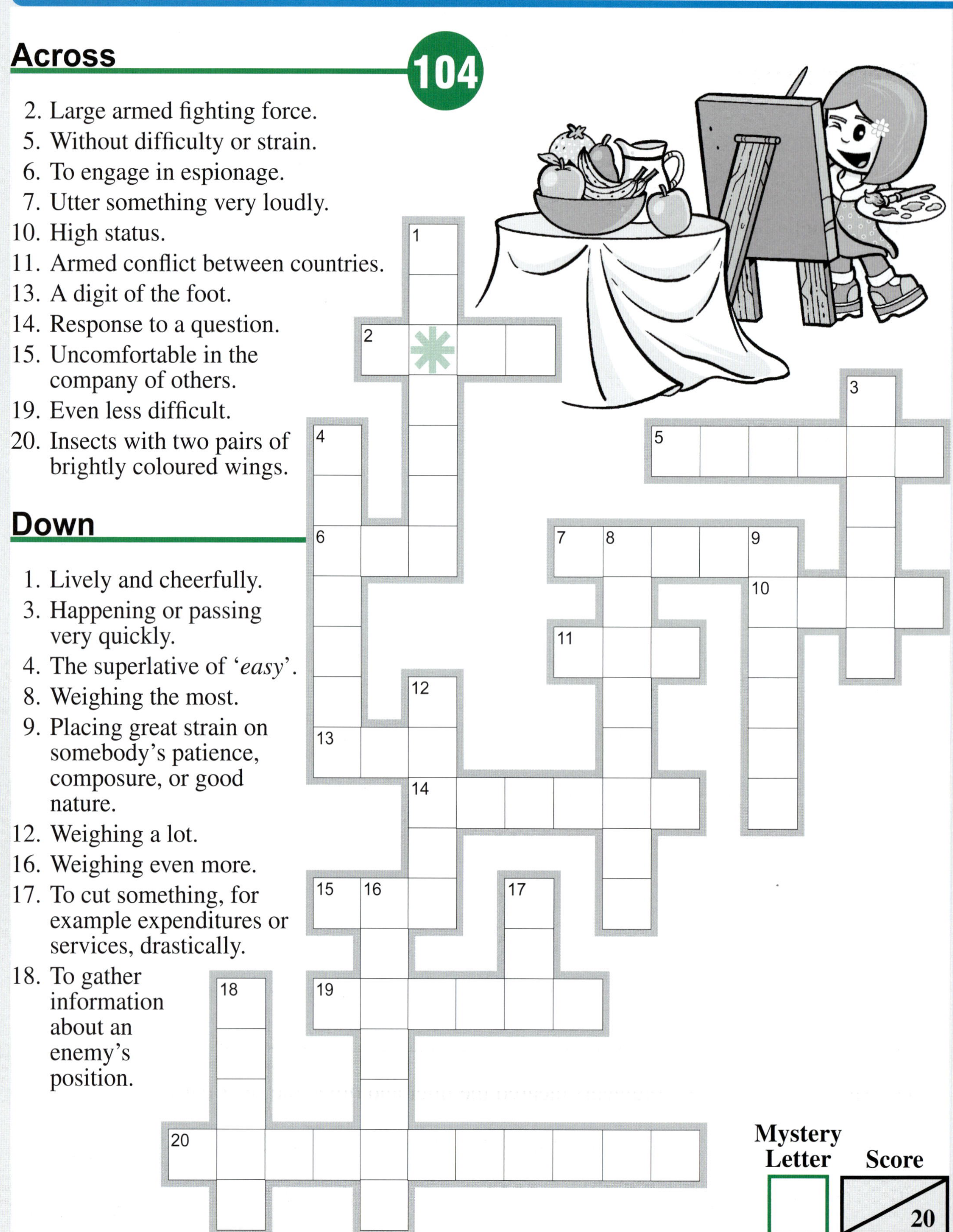

Mystery Letter

Score

20

heavy	**heavier**
heaviest	**war**
easier	**easiest**
easily	**merrily**

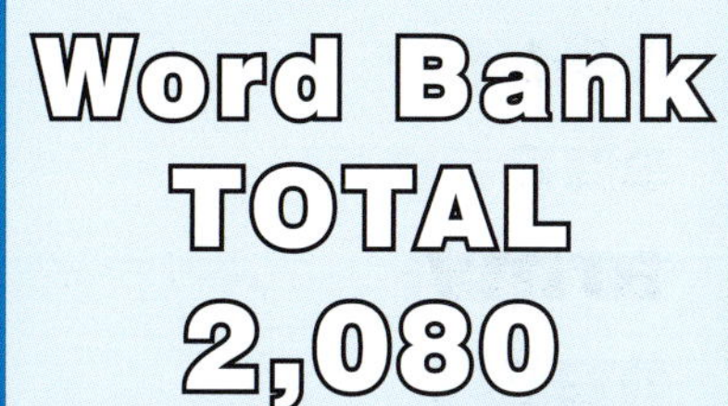

Exercise 104a

1) It is ____________ to climb up a ladder than it is to climb down.

2) Red Admiral ___________________ are found in Europe and North America.

3) The bucket was very ____________ when it was filled with water.

4) Mary spent the whole evening ___________ to finish her homework.

5) "Don't be _________ , come in and meet everyone."

6) The forestry worker used an __________ to fell the tree.

7) There were three routes up the mountain and they chose the ______________ .

8) The captain announced, "We shall be ____________ at an altitude of 28,000 feet".

9) She left the ________________ of the four bags for her husband to carry.

10) He was a _________ during the war and was tried for treason.

Score ___ / 10

Exercise 104b

11) The parcel weighed 18kg and was ______________ than the 15kg maximum limit.

12) The police sergeant was promoted to the ___________ of inspector.

13) He was walking round the house barefoot and stubbed his _________ on the table leg.

14) "There's no need to _____________ , I'm not deaf!"

15) The children were laughing and playing ______________ with each other.

16) The English Civil __________ began in 1642 and lasted for two years.

17) Looking through the telescope he could ___________ read the name on the ship's stern.

18) An ___________ of volunteers cleared the litter and tidied the river bank.

19) The _____________ Association was founded in 1908 by Lord Baden-Powell.

20) "The phone's ringing, could you _____________ it for me please."

Score ___ / 10

cause	**because**	**instant**
shadow	**arch**	**starch**
touch	**being**	**past**
mast	**fasten**	**odd**

Exercise 105a

1) The sailor climbed up the ship's ____________ to the crow's nest.

2) The vase shattered the ______________ it hit the floor.

3) Her parents waved _______________ from the station platform as the train departed.

4) He sent the letter and kept a ___________ of it for himself.

5) "Please ______________ your seat belts, the aeroplane is about to take off."

6) At the laundry, they used too much ____________ and the hotel sheets were very stiff.

7) The waiter poured the wine and waited for his customer to ___________ it.

8) They passed through the __________ and out onto the road.

9) "I'm afraid I can't help you ________________ we have no spare parts in stock."

10) She was rushing and, in her ____________ , she crashed the car.

Score /10

Exercise 105b

11) He had been very ill and was now only a ______________ of his former self.

12) The police raided the flat but it was ___________ and the suspects had disappeared.

13) She was tired of ___________ blamed for things that were not her fault.

14) "It's a __________ you aren't free, we would love to have you join us."

15) He had fallen a long way behind but there was ____________ of time left to catch up.

16) The rabbit's fur was soft to the ____________ and she stroked it affectionately.

17) They searched in vain for the key but it was a complete ____________ of time.

18) The investigators looked for clues to the ___________ of the rail crash.

19) She drove _____________ the junction and had to turn around.

20) He is a handyman and does __________ jobs for people.

Score /10

copy	**pity**
empty	**plenty**
taste	**waste**
haste	**goodbye**

Word Bank TOTAL 2,100

Across

105

1. Something that makes something happen.
3. Elapsed or gone by.
5. Feeling of sympathy for somebody else.
6. Unusual or peculiar.
10. Sense that identifies flavours.
11. Use something carelessly or without effect.
12. Stiffening substance for fabrics.
13. Vertical spar that supports sails, rigging or flags on a ship.
15. Existence.
16. Great speed.
19. For the reason that.

Down

1. One of many identical specimens.
2. Containing nothing.
4. Darkened shape of something.
7. An adequate or more than adequate amount.
8. Secure something or shut tightly.
9. Farewell.
14. Curved structure that forms the upper edge of an open space.
17. Feeling sense.
18. Happening immediately.

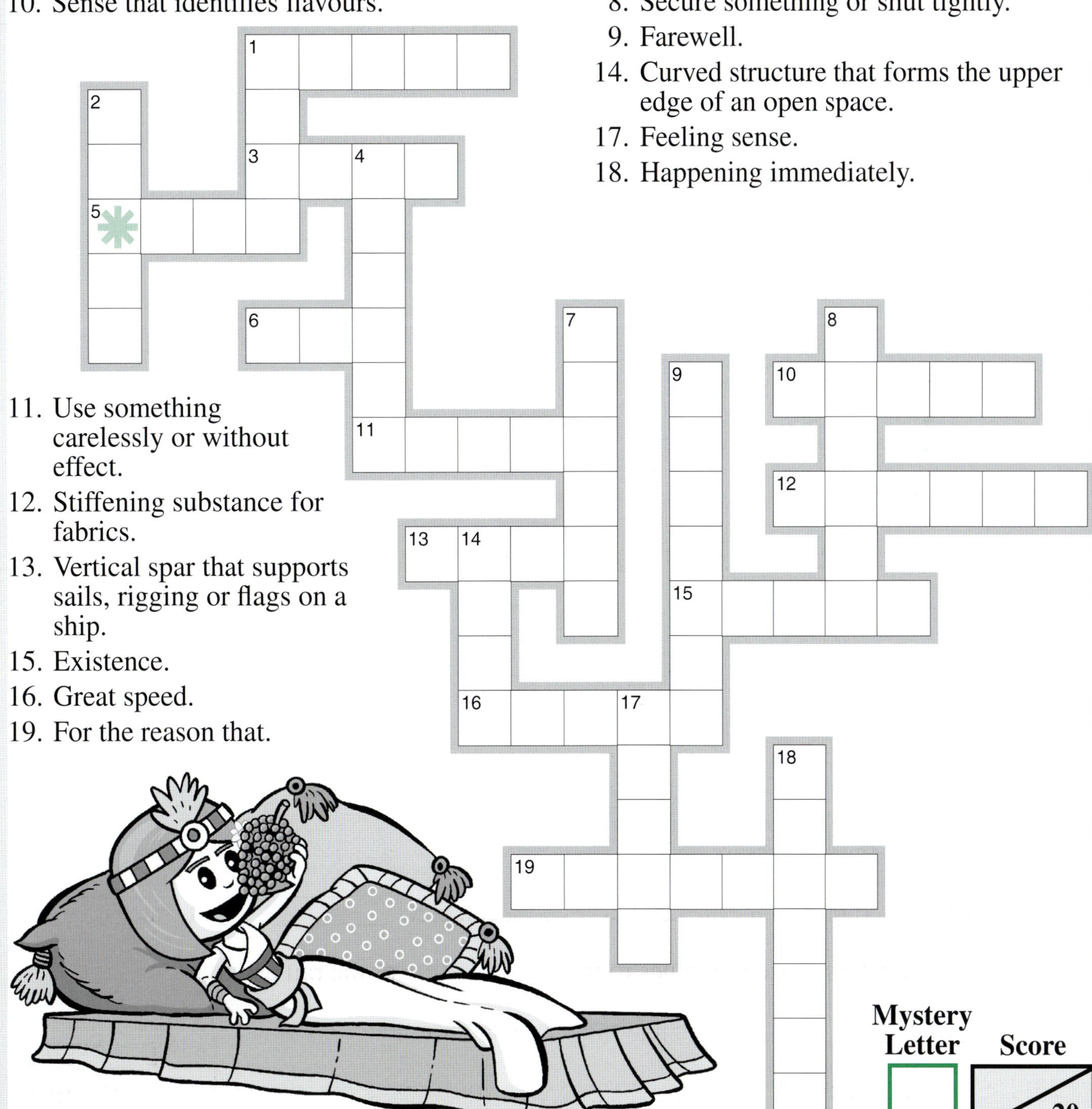

Mystery Letter

Score

20

loss	**lose**	**glory**
history	**manage**	**savage**
package	**postage**	**remind**
respond	**repent**	**record**

Across

106

1. To tell about what happened.
4. Organisation for maintaining law and order.
5. Violent, brutal, or undomesticated.
6. A piece cut from something.
10. To react.
12. The price paid for mail delivery.
14. What happened in the past.
16. The fame, admiration and honour given to somebody who does something important.
17. Join two pieces of rope by interweaving the strands of each into the other.
19. Send goods abroad.

Down

1. To cause a person to remember or think of something or somebody else.
2. To achieve something with difficulty.
3. To make a lasting account of something.
7. To recognise the wrong in something you have done and to be sorry about it.
8. The number 40.
9. To put things into a container or wrappings.
11. An announcement of information.
13. The amount of money by which a company's expenses exceed income.
15. Fail to win.
18. Bring in from abroad.

Mystery Letter

Score

20

slice	**splice**
notice	**police**
report	**import**
export	**forty**

Word Bank TOTAL 2,120

Exercise 106a

1) I bought some stamps to pay the ______________ on a parcel that I sent to Newcastle.

2) *Ali Baba and the* _____________ *Thieves* is a favourite children's story.

3) He was the Olympic Champion and revelled in the honour and the ____________ .

4) "You will have to ____________ me of the date: I have a terrible memory."

5) My company used to _____________ its products all over the world.

6) We ___________ many of the goods today that we used to manufacture ourselves.

7) I ______________ to make ends meet with only a very small pension.

8) He reported the theft of his bike to the _____________ .

9) The death of Sir Winston Churchill was a great __________ to the nation.

10) It was a ___________ attack and he was very badly injured.

Score ___ / 10

Exercise 106b

11) He promised to _____________ and mend his ways.

12) It was a difficult question to which he was unsure how to _______________ .

13) "He's showing off! Take no ____________ of him."

14) "Would you like a __________ of buttered toast with marmalade?"

15) She used a courier company to deliver the _______________ .

16) He was very angry but he tried to stay calm and not to ___________ his temper.

17) It was a detailed ___________ and left out none of the facts.

18) She set the video timer to ____________ this week's episode of her favourite serial.

19) The projectionist managed to ____________ together the two ends of the film.

20) He enjoyed learning about the past in _____________ lessons.

Score ___ / 10

rheumatism **accordion** **stationer** **secretary**
rhubarb **buccaneer** **detective** **fruitier**
tobacconist **confectioner** **ironmonger** **jeweller**

Exercise 107a

1) Her ____________________ worsened and her joints became stiffer.

2) A closed order of monks had lived in the __________________ for over nine centuries.

3) Engineers were fitting new cables to the electricity ___________ in the field.

4) "Would you like ice cream or custard with your _____________ crumble?"

5) It is an old-fashioned _____________________ 's shop that sells sweets from a jar.

6) The ____________________ had just the right hinges that my Dad needed.

7) She is an excellent ___________________ with a nose for a good story.

8) Their wedding reception was held in a ________________ in her parents' garden.

9) The National Trust restored the _________________ and it can grind flour once again.

10) The London Millennium ____________ housed an exhibition.

Score /10

Exercise 107b

11) The old man could no longer manage the stairs, so he bought a _________________ .

12) "This new orange cordial tastes much ________________ than the old one."

13) The old biplane was in the _______________ undergoing a full restoration.

14) The _______________ reset the diamond in her ring.

15) He plays the __________________ for a group of morris dancers.

16) His _________________ was ill and he had to type his own letters.

17) The ______________________ sold my Granddad a new pipe.

18) I like to read _________________ stories and to work out who committed the crime.

19) Many a __________________ preyed on ships in the West Indies in the 17th century.

20) She went to the ________________ 's to buy a new fountain pen.

Score /10

journalist	**windmill**
pylon	**dome**
hangar	**marquee**
bungalow	**monastery**

Word Bank TOTAL 2,140

Across

107

2. Maker or seller of sweets.
4. Somebody who investigates wrongdoing and gathers evidence.
5. Hemispherical roof.
6. A building with a set of wind-driven revolving sails or blades to drive a grinding machine.
10. Plant with green or pink leaf stalks that are edible when cooked.
12. Very large tent used for parties, meetings, sales and exhibitions.
14. A pirate.

Across (continued)

15. A seller of paper, envelopes, pens, pencils and other things used in writing.
16. Building housing aircraft.
17. Stiffness in joints and muscles.
18. Metal tower supporting high-voltage cables.
19. Someone who works as a writer or editor for a newspaper, magazine, or for radio or television.

Down

1. Someone who makes, sells or repairs jewellery.
3. Dealer in tools and other articles made chiefly of metal.
7. Person or shop that specialises in selling cigarettes, tobacco and pipes.
8. A monk's residence.
9. More reminiscent of fruit.
11. General clerical and administrative worker.
13. Air-driven musical instrument.
14. Single-storey house.

! Don't forget to go back to page **21** and complete **Kate's Mystery Word**.

Mystery Letter

Score 20

At the Dentist

Can you find all these words in the picture below? Write the correct word against each number. When you have finished you can colour in the picture if you want to.

chair **dental nurse** **syringe** **dentures** **tissues**
gloves **mouthwash** **tooth** **poster** **x-ray**
computer **basin** **instruments** **tunic** **jacket**

1.______________________ 2.______________________ 3.______________________

4.______________________ 5.______________________ 6.______________________

7.______________________ 8.______________________ 9.______________________

10.______________________ 11.______________________ 12.______________________

13.______________________ 14.______________________ 15.______________________

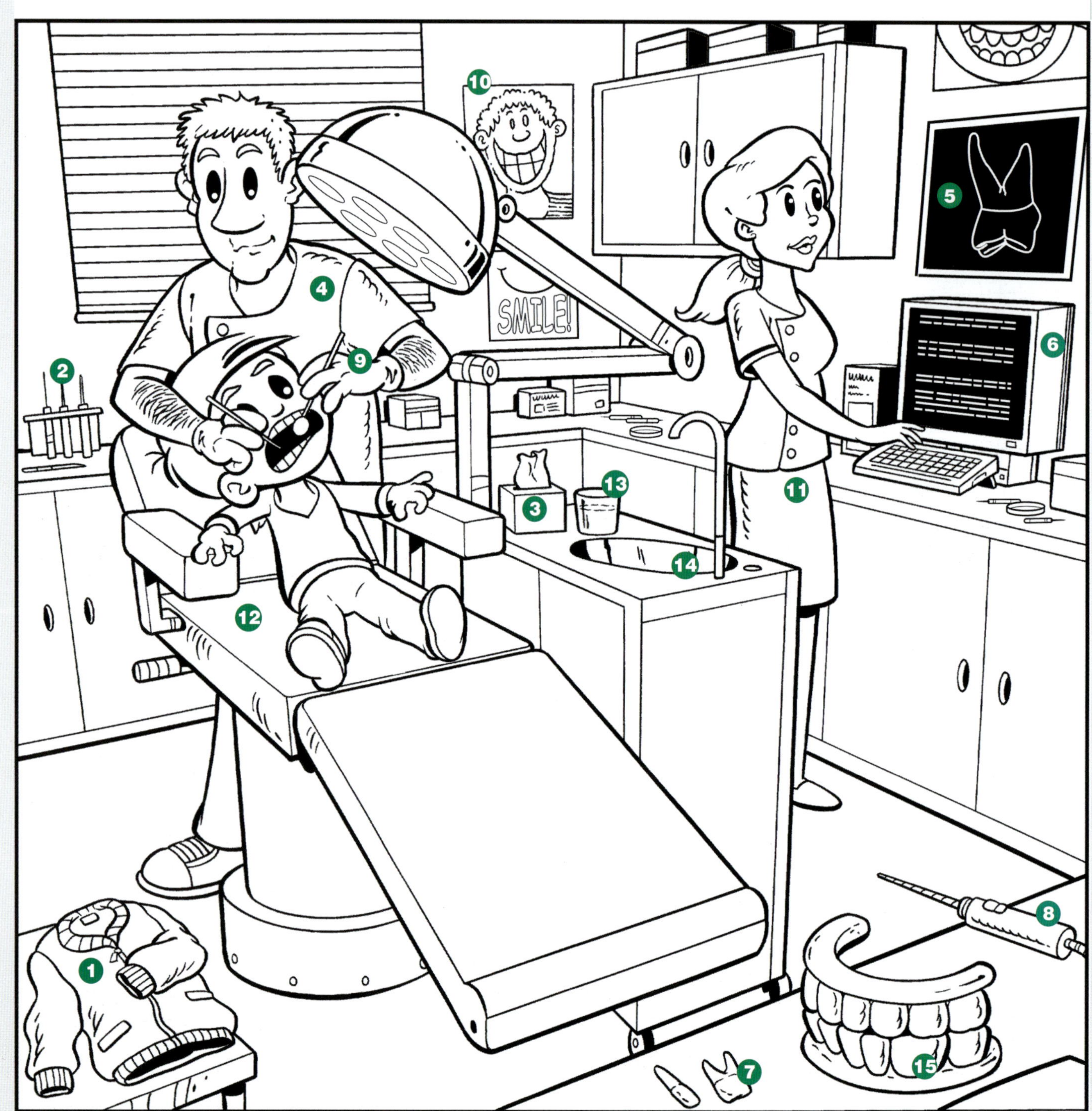

In the Accident & Emergency Department

Can you find all these words in the picture below? Write the correct word against each number.

chart	**doctor**	**ambulance**	**cylinder**	**pills**
stethoscope	**curtain**	**blanket**	**bandage**	**form**
patient	**seat**	**monitor**	**mattress**	**trolley**

1.____________ 2.____________ 3.____________

4.____________ 5.____________ 6.____________

7.____________ 8.____________ 9.____________

10.____________ 11.____________ 12.____________

13.____________ 14.____________ 15.____________

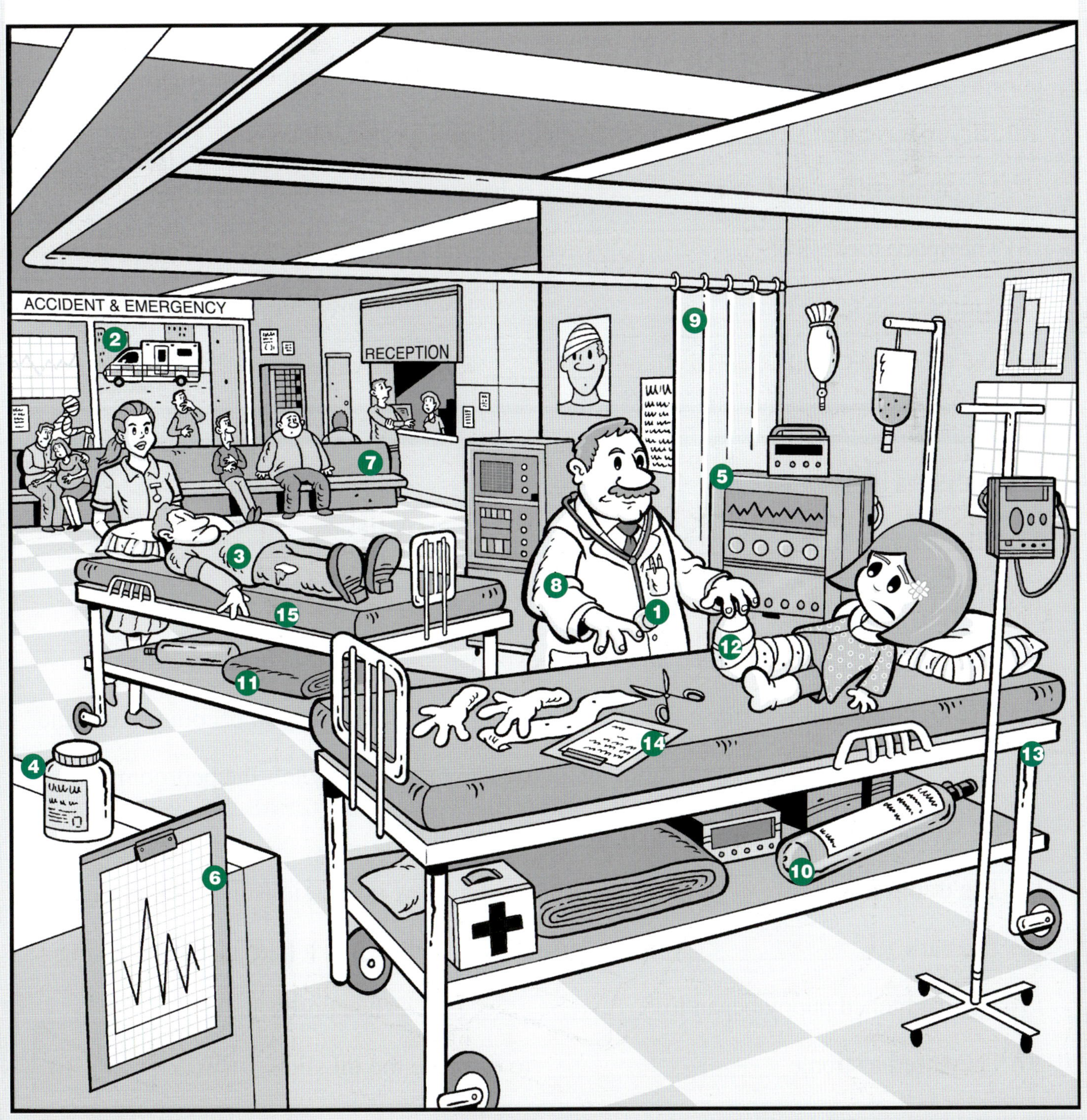

granary **abattoir** **restaurant**
cannibal **announcer** **penniless**
receipt **conceited** **democracy**
detergent **eighty** **honesty**

Exercise 108a

1) It had been a good harvest and the ________________ was full.

2) She was born in 1920 and was ______________ in the year 2000.

3) ______________________ falls around Whit Sunday: the seventh Sunday after Easter.

4) He is very __________________ and has an excessively high belief in his own ability.

5) The _____________________ 's voice boomed out from the public address system.

6) "If you have the _______________ for the purchase, I can exchange the goods."

7) My auntie plays cards at a ______________ drive every Wednesday afternoon.

8) The space rocket's ________________ increased rapidly as it climbed towards the stars.

9) Animals are taken to an _________________ to be slaughtered humanely.

10) My Granddad drinks Scotch _______________ with soda water.

Score / 10

Exercise 108b

11) All the tables in the ___________________ were full, so they had to eat elsewhere.

12) In a ____________________ people elect their representatives to govern them.

13) The ________________ killed and ate the explorer.

14) The first time that you ride a bike it is a ______________ but it soon becomes mundane.

15) She ___________________ 'goodnight' to her baby and quietly left the bedroom.

16) He returned the purse she dropped and she admired his ________________ .

17) The tramp was ___________________ and kept his few possessions in a carrier bag.

18) The cat's __________________ were covered with milk when it had finished drinking.

19) The frightened puppy began to __________________ as he approached it.

20) They used a strong ___________________ to disperse the oil slick.

Score / 10

velocity
whist
Whitsuntide
whimper

novelty
whiskers
whisky
whispered

Word Bank TOTAL 2,160

Across

108

1. Somebody who provides informative comment on something.
5. Truthfulness.
7. Alcoholic beverage made from fermented grain.
9. Sob softly.
12. Very poor or without any money.
14. Newness and originality.
16. The control of an organisation by all of its members.
17. The days around Whit Sunday.
18. Someone who eats human flesh.
19. A cleansing substance that dissolves dirt and oil.

Down

2. An eating place.
3. Hair growing near an animal's mouth.
4. A place where animals are slaughtered.
6. Eight times ten.
7. A card game that is the forerunner of bridge.
8. Spoke or suggested something in a confidential or furtive manner.
10. Acknowledgement that something has been received.
11. Grain warehouse.
13. Too proud.
15. Speed.

1 2 3 4 5 6 7 8 9 10 11 12 13 14 15 16 17 18 19

Put the mystery letters from the starred squares (✳) in puzzles **108** to **115** into their numbered box below, then rearrange them to make **Oliver's Mystery Word**.

The clue is **FUEL**.

Enter your mystery letters here:

108 109 110 111 112 113 114 115

Now rearrange them to make the:

Mystery Word:

smoulder **rocket** **peregrine** **maggot**

boulder **clipper** **hare** **begging**

athlete **motorcycle** **luggage** **leggings**

Across

109

1. Slanting or oblique.
2. Large rock.
6. Protective covering for the lower leg.
9. Worm-shaped insect lava.
10. Leaves of a plant or tree.
11. Asking for something in a very intense, humble, or even humiliating way.
12. A competitor in track-and-field events.
13. Oval tissue mass in the back of the mouth, important for the body's immune system.

Across (continued)

14. A thin sheet of material with a cut-out design.
15. Large fast-running member of the rabbit family.
16. Fast mid-19th-century tall sailing ship.
17. Space vehicle.

Down

1. Springtime plant with yellow trumpet-shaped flowers.
3. Suitcases and bags used during a journey.
4. Long narrow sledge without runners.
5. A two-wheeled road vehicle powered by an engine.
6. Plant of the pea family with edible seeds.
7. Tool or container.
8. Coming from another region or country, wandering or travelling.
14. Burn slowly.

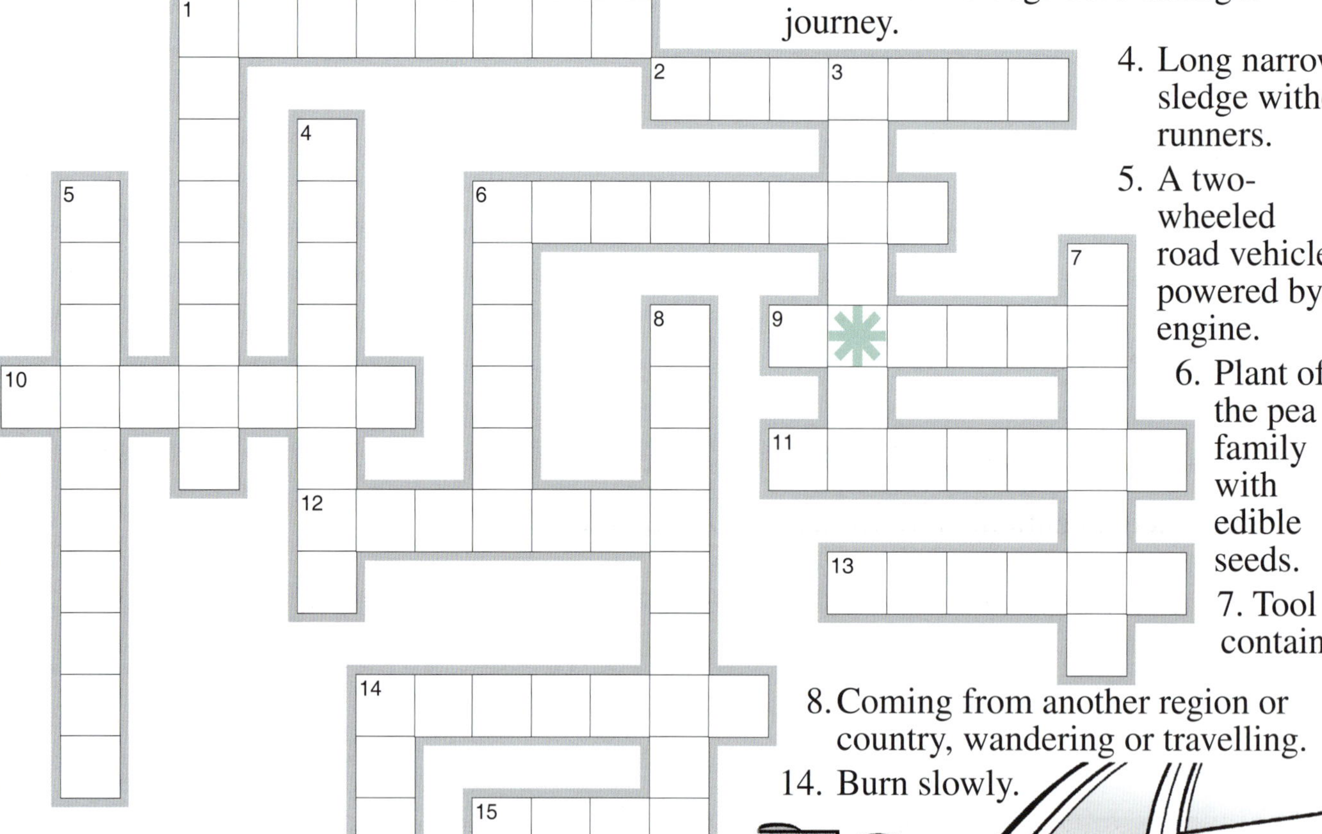

Mystery Letter

Score /20

toboggan	**tonsil**
lentil	**stencil**
utensil	**daffodil**
foliage	**diagonal**

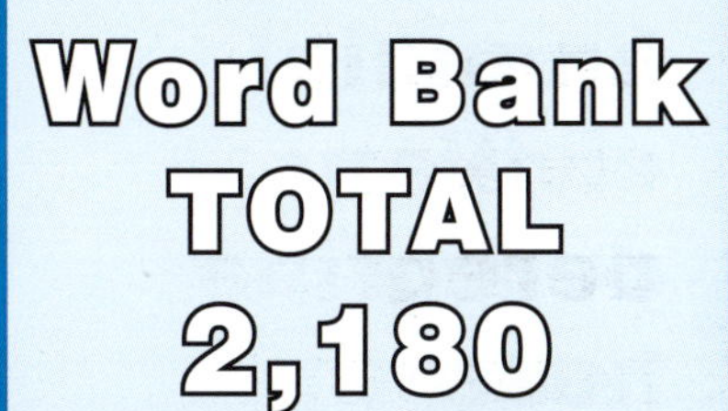

Exercise 109a

1) A __________ stopped, sat bolt-upright, listened with his large ears and then ran off.

2) A box junction is denoted by __________________ yellow lines painted on the road.

3) He raced down the snow-covered hill on his ___________________ .

4) The _______________________ courier weaved his machine through the heavy traffic.

5) The Welsh celebrate St David's day by wearing a _______________ .

6) A huge _______________ had fallen from the cliff and rolled across the promenade.

7) The __________________ falcon's rapid downward stoop with closed wings is remarkable.

8) A colander is a kitchen ________________ used to drain food cooked in water.

9) Orang-utans live and hide in the thick ______________ of forest trees.

10) The bonfire continued to __________________ for several hours.

Score /10

Exercise 109b

11) A ___________ is either of the two small oval tissue masses at the back of the mouth.

12) She asked a gentleman to lift her suitcase onto the _______________ rack.

13) A ______________ engine's thrust is produced by expelling expanding hot gases.

14) Chaps are protective leather _________________ worn on horseback by cowboys.

15) He reeled in his fishing line and put a new fly ________________ on the hook.

16) You must follow an intensive training regime to be a top track or field ______________ .

17) They sprayed 'HANDLE WITH CARE' on the packing case using a _______________ .

18) The orphaned children were ________________ on the streets of Calcutta.

19) She made a tasty ______________ soup that was rich in protein.

20) The *Cutty Sark* is perhaps the best known ______________ .

Score /10

financial	**valiant**	**diameter**
civilians	**dignified**	**satisfied**
defied	**crucified**	**magnified**
hose	**firemen**	**ambulance**

Exercise 110a

1) She was very seriously ill but made a ____________________ recovery.

2) He connected the sprinkler to the ____________ and watered the lawn.

3) The box contained a collection of _________________________ motorcycle parts.

4) They dialled 999 and an _____________________ arrived several minutes later.

5) Several ________________ wearing breathing apparatus entered the burning building.

6) Many ________________ were killed in air raids during the London Blitz.

7) He was very brave and made a _________________ attempt to rescue the children.

8) Mummy took me to the hospital's _________________ department when I fell over.

9) Not ________________ with only one sweet, the child took three more!

10) The plumber measured the __________________ of the pipe.

Score ___ / 10

Exercise 110b

11) The Harrier jump jet ____________ gravity and hovered five metres above the ground.

12) Running round and round the track became very boring and ____________________ .

13) The strand of human hair, _________________ under the microscope, looked like string.

14) The Lords looked very ________________ as their procession entered Parliament.

15) He recounted a very __________________ anecdote and the audience laughed.

16) The jury all agreed and returned a ____________________ verdict.

17) For Halloween the children wore ______________ masks of vampires and ghouls.

18) The ________________ markets closed with the dollar weaker against the pound.

19) It was a ___________ and nerve-racking moment as he prepared to bungee jump.

20) Jesus Christ was _________________ on the cross at Calvary.

Score ___ / 10

casualty
miraculous
unanimous
miscellaneous
tense
hideous
monotonous
humorous

Word Bank TOTAL 2,200

Across

110

2. Totally unexpected, extraordinary and marvellous.
6. People employed to extinguish fires.
7. Contented or pleased.
9. Line through the centre of a circle.
13. Witty or funny.
15. Composed of many varied things that have no necessary connection with each other.
17. Agreed on by everyone.
18. Connected with money.
19. Showing self-respect.

Down

1. Worried or nervous and not relaxed.
3. Ordinary citizens and not the armed forces.
4. Horrible to see.
5. Challenged authority or power and refused to obey.
8. Executed by crucifixion.
10. Flexible tube or pipe.
11. Repetitious and uninteresting.
12. Courageous or brave.
14. Accident victim.
15. Increased the apparent size.
16. Vehicle for carrying people to and from hospital.

Mystery Letter

Score

20

anonymous **foremost** **forecast**
forearm **foreman** **merciful**
colourful **dreadful** **tasteful**
painful **painfully** **dolefully**

Across

111

4. Man in charge of other workers.
9. In a way that corresponds to fact or reality, or that expresses the truth.
11. Lower arm between the elbow and the wrist.
13. In a manner very pleasing to the senses.
14. Laboriously or embarrassingly badly.
17. Unnamed.
18. Producing great fear or awe.
19. Nearest to the front.
20. Very sadly and mournfully.

Down

1. Happily and optimistically.
2. Interesting and exciting.
3. Showing good aesthetic taste.
5. Great physical strength and energy.
6. Hurting as a result of an injury or disease.
7. A shape's outline.
8. Magnificence.
10. In a manner authorised or permitted by the law.
12. Showing compassion.
15. With a protective metal covering.
16. Predict what will happen.

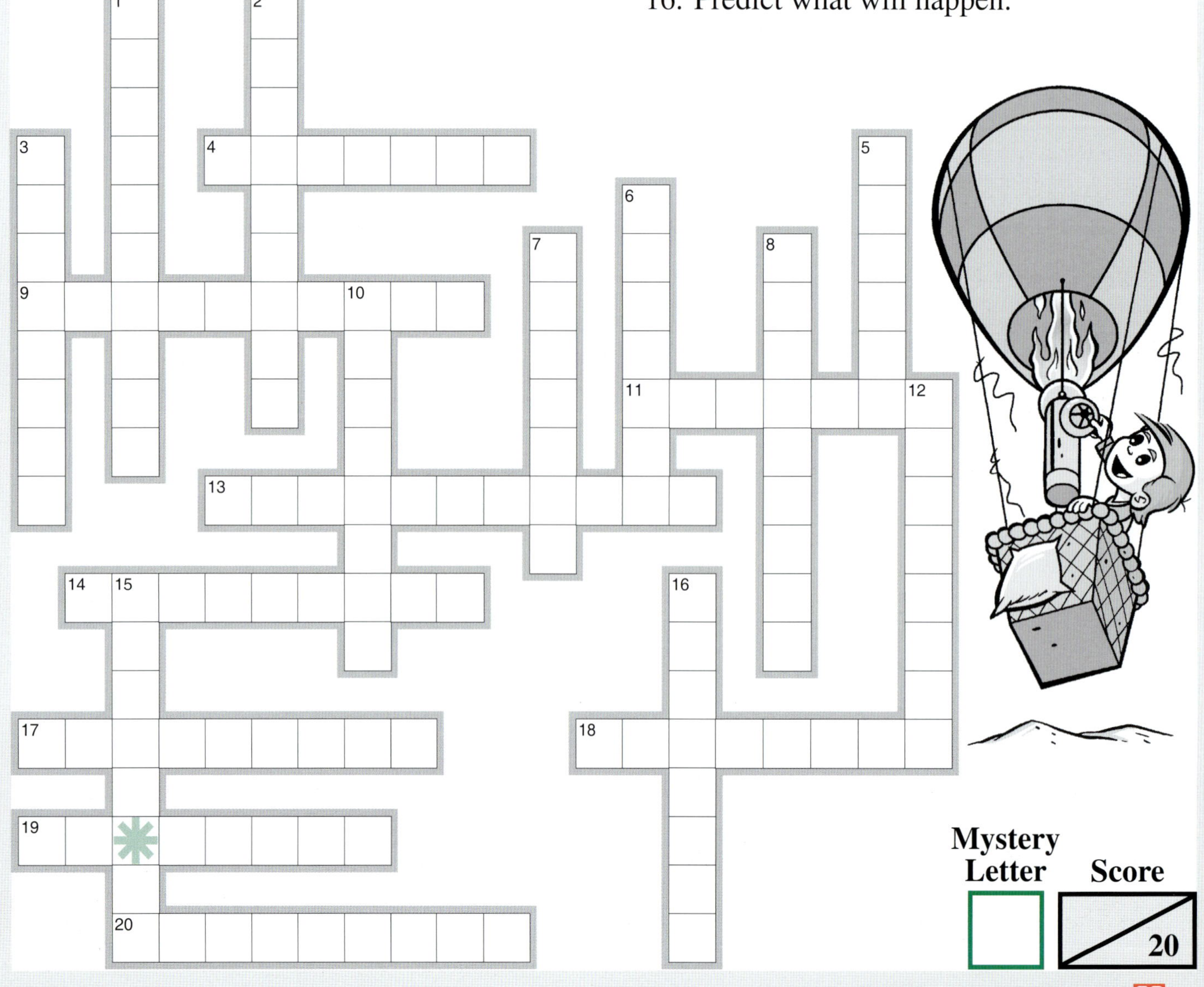

beautifully
lawfully
vigour
contour
cheerfully
truthfully
splendour
armoured

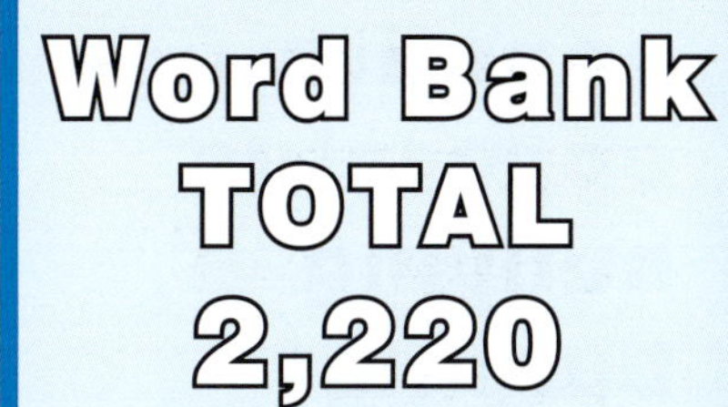

Exercise 111a

1) It was an ________________ letter without an address or signature.

2) The ________________ security van collected the supermarket's daily takings.

3) He went to the dentist because he had a very ____________ abscess under his tooth.

4) The flowers that they had planted made a very ______________ display.

5) By studying the map's _____________ lines, he knew that the hill was very steep.

6) The room was decorated _________________ with gilded bosses on the ceiling.

7) The young shoots grew with _____________ and soon needed to be cut back.

8) Rain was ________________ for the weekend, so she cancelled the barbecue.

9) He made a _______________ mistake which he regretted for the rest of his life.

10) The _______________ gave instructions to the factory workers.

Score ___ / 10

Exercise 111b

11) He had always lived his life _____________ and everyone was shocked by his crime.

12) The mourners at her funeral stood _______________ at the graveside.

13) The interior of the Russian palace exuded opulence and _________________ .

14) Our milkman seemed very happy and came up the path whistling _______________ .

15) He stowed the crate towards the front in the ______________ section of the hold.

16) The patients were treated by ______________ and compassionate nuns.

17) The karate black belt used his _____________ to parry the blow.

18) The decor is very _____________ with velvet drapes and matching soft furnishings.

19) His knee was injured and he limped ________________ off the pitch.

20) She was under oath and gave her evidence ________________ .

Score ___ / 10

appetite	**appalling**	**apprentice**
apparatus	**worrying**	**hurrying**
bullying	**copying**	**replying**
burying	**denying**	**pitying**

Exercise 112a

1) The rain continued to ______________ and they had to stay indoors all day.

2) His business was expanding so he took on a young ___________________ to train.

3) Jack was always good at sport but he used to ____________ at tennis.

4) "Pass the tomato _______________ , I want to put some on my chips."

5) The __________________ in the gymnasium was old and needed replacing.

6) The older boys were caught _________________ and threatening the younger boys.

7) My dog is always digging holes and ______________ things in the garden.

8) She opened the vacuum ____________ and poured out a hot drink for each of them.

9) Everyone was _______________ along the road so as not to be late for the match.

10) Children learn how to do things by _______________ others.

Score /10

Exercise 112b

11) It was an _________________ mess with twisted metal and broken glass everywhere.

12) His face showed he was angry and he continued to ____________ at the boys.

13) Dick Fosbury developed the high jump technique known as the 'Fosbury _________ '.

14) "When _______________ to the advertisement, please send two photographs."

15) If you eat snacks between meals you will spoil your ______________ .

16) The strong breeze made the tall plane trees ______________ gently to and fro.

17) "It's useless _____________ that you were there, you were seen by three people."

18) He is always ________________ about everything and never enjoys himself.

19) "Don't spend your time ______________ somebody. Try to help them!"

20) It was a complete mystery and it continued to ___________ her.

Score /10

excel	**baffle**
scowl	**flask**
sway	**drizzle**
flop	**ketchup**

Word Bank TOTAL 2,240

Across

112

4. Thick savoury sauce, usually made with tomatoes, that is served cold as a condiment.
7. Digging a hole, putting something in it, and then replacing the soil.
8. Sit or lie down heavily.
10. A frown expressing anger, displeasure, or menace.
11. To swing back and forth.
14. Declaring that something is not true.
17. Making an identical version.
18. Dreadful or shocking.
19. Trainee learning an art, craft, or trade as a profession.

Down

1. Feeling sadness because somebody else is in trouble or pain.
2. Rushing.
3. Equipment used for a particular purpose.
5. Responding to what somebody says.
6. A small glass bottle.
7. Intimidating a weaker person.
9. Being or making anxious.
12. To do better than all others or than a given standard.
13. Light steady rain.
15. To puzzle somebody.
16. Natural desire for food.

planet	**quintuplets**	**scotch**
cider	**jogging**	**oxygen**
droop	**squaw**	**scrabble**
pounce	**stray**	**bleach**

113

Across

4. Alcoholic drink made from apples.
7. Colourless, odourless gas, necessary for combustion and animal respiration.
11. Animal's nose and jaws.
12. To jump suddenly onto something.
13. Running at a moderate pace as exercise.
16. Walking aids.
18. Whisky produced in Scotland.
19. Native North American woman or wife.
20. Close and reopen both eyes rapidly.

Down

1. To produce bubbles of gas.
2. Hang or bend down limply.
3. Five offspring borne to one mother from a single pregnancy.
5. Moving something rapidly to and fro.
6. Astronomical body orbiting a star.
8. Chemical substance that removes colour.
9. Almost asleep.
10. Shine with a flicker.
14. Grope about frantically in an effort to find something.
15. Enormous.
17. Wander away.

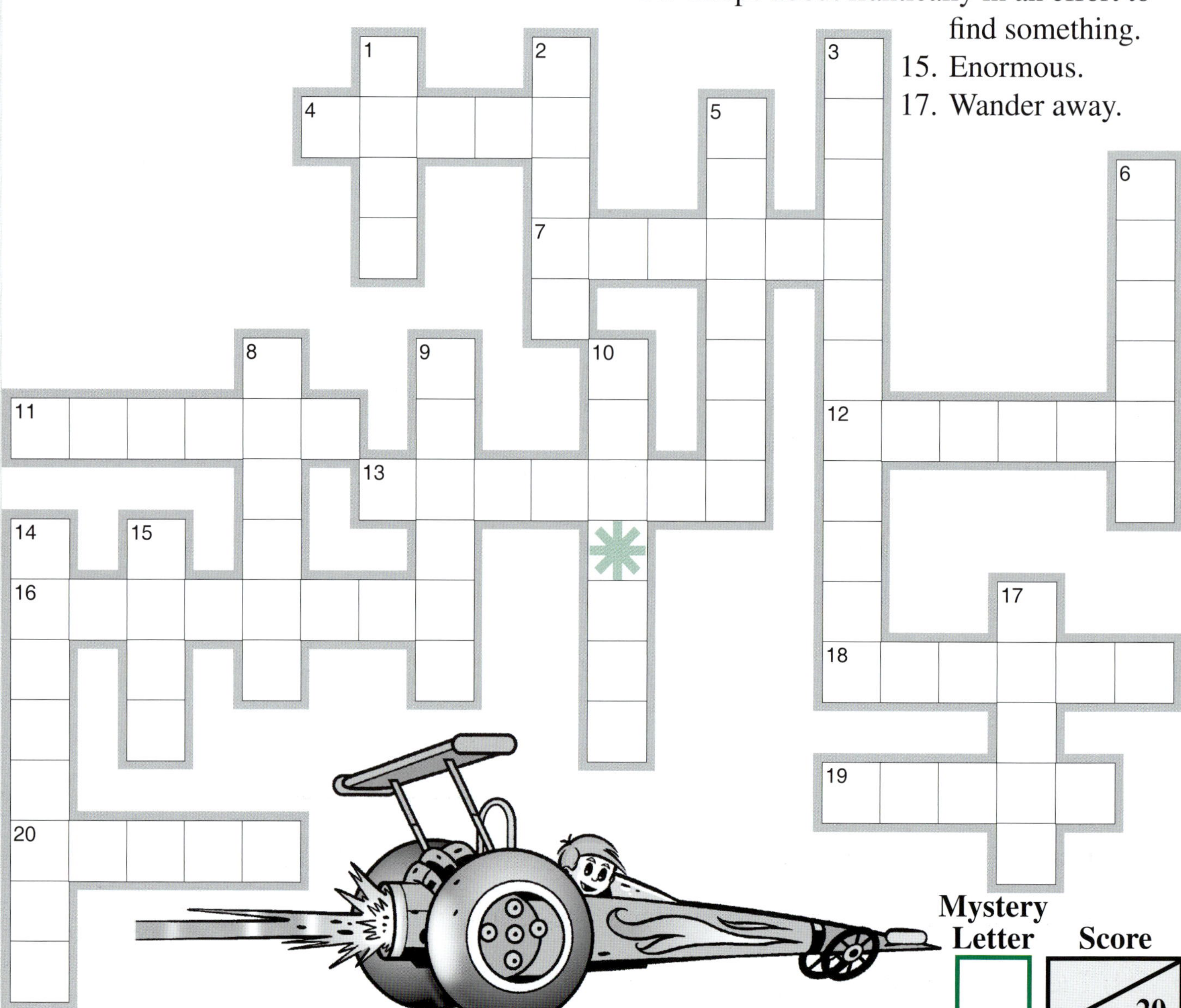

huge
wagging
fizz
muzzle
twinkle
drowsy
crutches
blink

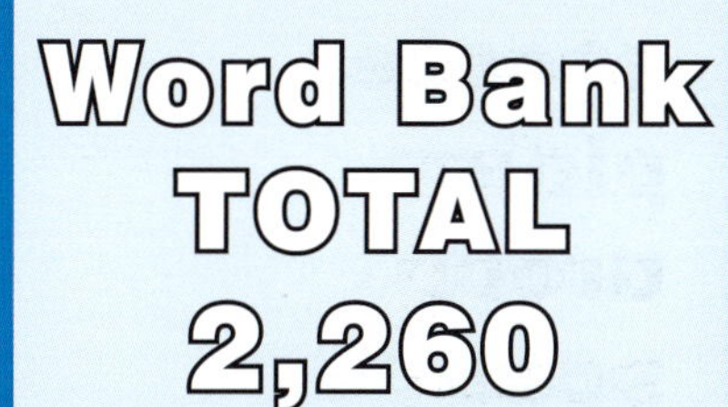

Exercise 113a

1) His rifle had just been discharged and its _______________ was still smoking.

2) A fire needs three elements: fuel, heat and _____________ .

3) He saw the North Star _______________ in the cold night sky.

4) She had to ________________ around on the floor to retrieve the dropped coins.

5) The company issued a press release to ______________ rumours about its demise.

6) She accidentally splashed ______________ on her blouse and it removed the colour.

7) She put her ear nearer to the glass and could hear the _________ of the lemonade.

8) She gave birth to _____________________ and they had to buy five of everything.

9) While his leg was in plaster, he got around on ________________ .

10) Jupiter is the largest _______________ in the solar system.

Score ___ / 10

Exercise 113b

11) He found an old book that referred to a Native American's wife as his ______________ .

12) The friends go _______________ together in the park in order to keep fit.

13) The West Country is renowned for producing _________ from pressed apples.

14) "Stay near me and don't ___________ too far or we may lose each other."

15) The nurse told her to ___________ rapidly to remove the grit from her eye.

16) He was very tired and began to feel ______________ .

17) A _____________ wave, over five metres tall, crashed over the ship's deck.

18) Her dog was very pleased to see her and was _________________ its tail.

19) With a sudden ______________ , the cat leapt onto its prey.

20) The flowers began to ____________ through lack of water.

Score ___ / 10

scooter	**hiss**	**florist**
plaice	**dandruff**	**screech**
twist	**sizzle**	**bigger**
scab	**tandoori**	**stride**

Exercise 114a

1) Long after the accident, her skin was still discoloured from all the ______________ .

2) His mother bought him a new shampoo to try to prevent his ______________ .

3) My father ______________ the train at seven forty-five each weekday morning.

4) She ordered ______________ chicken with rice at the local Indian restaurant.

5) He bought a ______________ from the bookshop to read on the train.

6) She ordered a wreath for her friend's funeral from the local ______________ .

7) "Mum wants cod, Dad wants skate and I'll have ___________ from the chip shop."

8) Mandy's boyfriend rides a motor ______________ and she rides pillion.

9) The class learnt their ______________ tables by rote.

10) The bacon began to ____________ noisily in the frying pan.

Score /10

Exercise 114b

11) He badly grazed his knee when he fell off his bike and a large _________ formed.

12) "That's the ______________ pig I've ever seen!"

13) All the items with that particular ___________ number had to be rejected.

14) The lane continued to __________ and turn for several miles.

15) The steam engine came to a sudden stop with a loud ______________ of brakes.

16) He continued to blow and the balloon got _____________ .

17) It would have worried most people but Graham took it all in his ___________ .

18) He could hear the _________ of escaping air and he knew that the tyre was punctured.

19) No ______________ of money can ever buy you happiness.

20) "Mind your __________ when you get off the bus."

Score /10

amount
multiplication
step
bruising
fattest
batch
paperback
catches

Word Bank TOTAL 2,280

Across

114

5. Thickest or widest.
7. Of greater size, number, or amount.
10. Make a sound like a continuous *'s'*.
11. Someone who owns or works in a shop that sells flowers.
13. A hissing and splattering sound typical of food frying.
14. Takes hold of something that is travelling through the air.
17. Two-wheeled child's toy.
18. A quantity or degree of something.

Down

1. Marinated then baked or cooked in a clay oven *(tandoor)*.
2. Walk along briskly with long regular steps.
3. Arithmetic operation symbolised by 'x'.
4. The crust over a healing wound.
6. To make one end turn in the opposite direction to the other.
7. Discoloration of the skin surface.
8. Large, edible, flat-bodied seafish that has brown skin with red or orange spots.
9. A softcover book.
12. Dry scales of dead skin that are shed from the scalp.
15. A high pitched grating sound.
16. The amount of material produced in one operation.
17. A stage in a progression towards some goal or target.

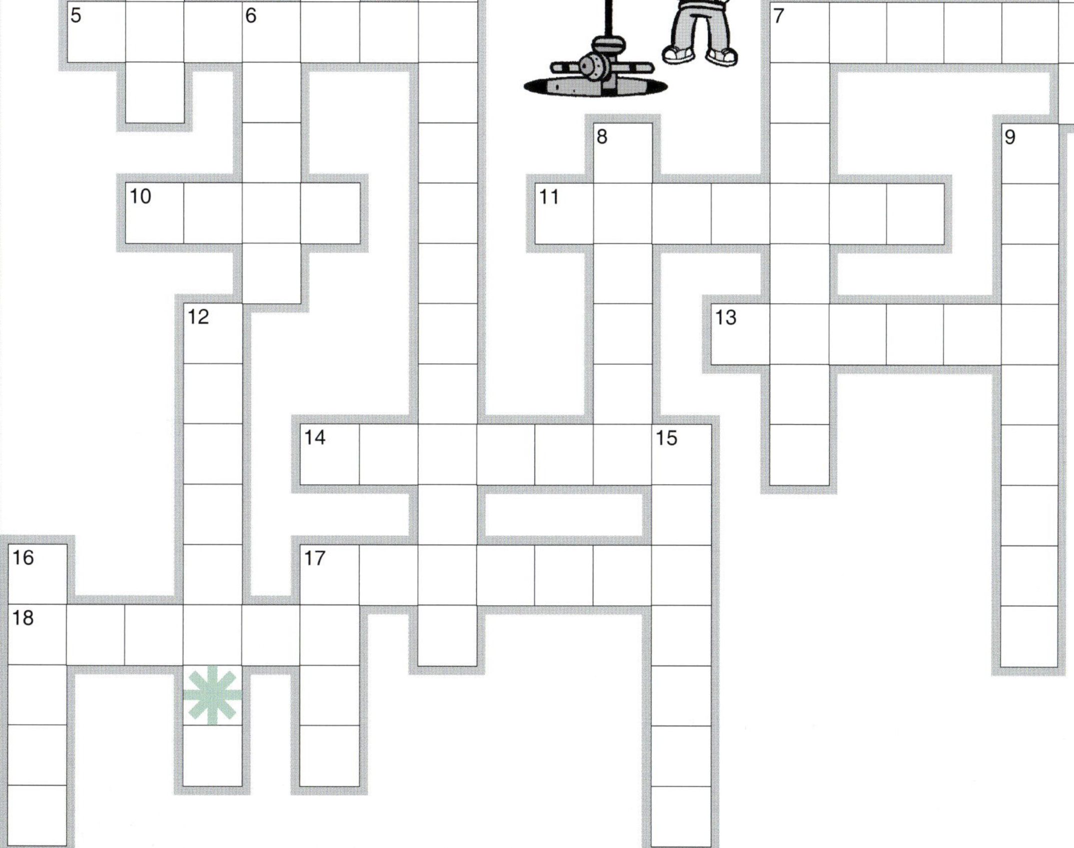

Mystery Letter

Score

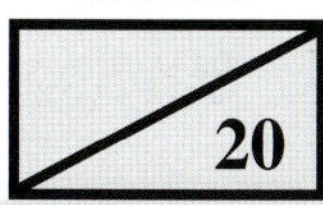

pawn	**circled**	**sunshine**
cleanest	**qualify**	**taller**
comment	**thatched**	**thirst**
counts	**saddest**	**sharpest**

Exercise 115a

1) Her washing machine was not _______________ properly, so she called an engineer.

2) They spent a relaxing week ________________ along the canal on a narrowboat.

3) His height is 1.9 metres and William is _____________ than all his classmates.

4) The chess player moved his _____________ diagonally and took his opponent's knight.

5) The ______________ on either side of the road filled with water during a monsoon.

6) The ________________ General advises the government on English law.

7) The police chief did not reply when asked to _________________ on the events.

8) Solar, tidal and wind power are some of the ________________ energy sources.

9) After another breach in security, the airport procedures were found _______________ .

10) The pack of hyenas ______________ around the stricken zebra.

Score /10

Exercise 115b

11) It was very pleasant in the ________________ but much cooler in the shade.

12) In my school, a lot of __________________ was placed on sport and drama.

13) It was one of the _______________ days of his life when his best friend emigrated.

14) In historical romantic novels, a woman's ___________ tries to persuade her to marry him.

15) To quench her ____________ she drank a large, cold glass of fresh orange juice.

16) As it got ______________ it became impossible to read the map without a torch.

17) "Status _____________ for nothing here: we judge everyone on their merit."

18) She was extremely sarcastic and critical with the ________________ tongue imaginable.

19) It is a pretty village in which all the cottages have ________________ roofs.

20) She was fourth in her heat but failed to _____________ for the final.

Score /10

cruising
darker
ditches
emphasis
wanting
suitor
attorney
working

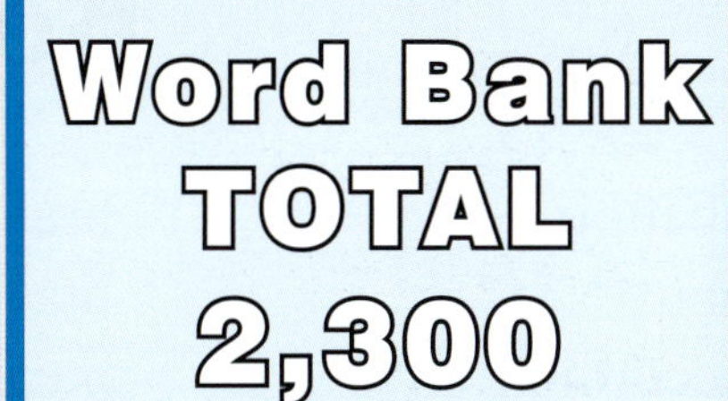

Across

115

4. Remark or observation.
6. Says numbers in order usually starting at one.
9. Unhappiest.
11. To become eligible for a position or privilege.
12. Most able to cut.
14. Chess piece of the lowest value.
15. Travelling by sea on a pleasure trip.
17. Not lighter.
18. Considerably higher.

Down

1. Special importance, significance, or stress.
2. Somebody legally empowered by a document to make decisions and act on behalf of somebody else.
3. Least dirty.
4. Drew a ring around.
5. A desire or need to drink liquid.
7. Not meeting expectations or requirements.
8. Somebody on whose behalf a case is brought to a law court.
10. Roofed with straw or rushes.
12. Direct sunlight.
13. Long narrow drainage channels dug in the ground.
16. Capable of being used or operated.

1 2 3 4 5 6 7 8 9 10 11 12 13 14 15 16 17 18

Don't forget to go back to page **37** and complete **Oliver's Mystery Word**.

Mystery Letter **Score** 20

Book Five Word List

abattoir
above
accordion
afraid
afternoon
afterwards
alike
aloud
ambulance
amount
announcer
anonymous
answer
appalling
apparatus
appetite
apprentice
arch
armoured
army
around
athlete
attorney
axe
baffle
batch
battle
beautifully
because
begging
being
between
bigger
birth
birthday
bitter
bleach
blink
bloom
border
bottle
boulder
boxes
branch

branches
bravely
breakfast
brighter
brightest
bruising
buccaneer
build
building
built
bullying
bungalow
burnt
burying
butterflies
calf
cannibal
capture
casualty
catches
cattle
cause
chance
cheer
cheerfully
chew
chief
Christmas
cider
circled
civilians
classes
clay
cleanest
cling
clipper
cloak
coal
colourful
comment
conceited
confectioner
content
contour

cooler
copper
copy
copying
cork
counts
creeping
crew
crucified
cruising
crutches
cuff
cure
daffodil
daisies
daisy
dandruff
darker
darkness
deaf
deed
deeper
defend
defied
democracy
denying
detective
detergent
diagonal
diameter
dignified
dishes
ditches
dolefully
dome
dread
dreadful
drizzle
droop
drowsy
dwell
dying
earn
earth

easier
easiest
easily
Easter
eighty
eleven
emphasis
empty
excel
export
fasten
fattest
fence
fifteen
fifth
fifty
financial
finer
finger
finish
fir
firemen
fixed
fizz
flame
flask
flesh
flew
float
flock
flop
florist
flying
foliage
forearm
forecast
foreman
foremost
forest
forty
forward
four
fourteen
fourth

Book Five Word List

frame
friend
fruitier
gift
glasses
glory
goodbye
grace
granary
grandmother
grey
grief
grind
half
halves
hangar
hare
haste
heaven
heavier
heaviest
heavy
hideous
hiding
hiss
history
honesty
hoping
hose
however
huge
humorous
hundred
hurry
hurrying
husband
illness
import
inches
indeed
instant
invite
ironmonger
jail

jeweller
jogging
journalist
ketchup
kettle
knee
kneel
knife
knives
knock
knot
lawfully
leaves
leggings
lemon
lentil
lilies
lily
loaf
loaves
lose
loss
luggage
lying
maggot
magnified
mail
manage
manner
marquee
mast
matter
merciful
merrily
miner
miraculous
miscellaneous
monastery
monotonous
motorcycle
move
multiplication
muzzle
nearly

notice
novelty
odd
order
oxygen
package
paid
painful
painfully
paperback
past
pawn
peach
peaches
penniless
pepper
peregrine
person
picture
pint
pity
pitying
plaice
planet
plenty
poem
poet
police
postage
pounce
present
pretend
price
prove
provide
pure
pylon
qualify
quickly
quiet
quintuplets
rail
raise
raised

rank
rate
rattle
receipt
record
remark
remind
remove
repair
repeat
repent
replying
report
respond
restaurant
rheumatism
rhubarb
roam
roast
rocket
saddest
safer
safest
satisfied
savage
scab
scooter
scotch
scout
scowl
scrabble
scrape
screech
secretary
serve
shadow
sharpest
shelf
shining
should
shout
shy
silly
simple

Book Five Word List

since
sixteen
sixty
sizzle
skate
skating
slice
slipped
smiling
smoulder
snail
soak
soap
sore
space
spider
splendour
splice
spy
squaw
starch
starve
stationer
steel
steep
stencil
step

stiff
stray
stride
strike
strip
stuff
sugar
suitor
sunshine
sure
sway
swimming
taller
tandoori
taste
tasteful
tenth
term
tense
thatched
themselves
thief
thieves
thirst
thirteen
thirty
thousand

threw
thrown
tie
tied
tired
tobacconist
toboggan
toe
together
tonsil
touch
towards
track
trunk
truthfully
trying
twelve
twenty
twice
twinkle
twist
unanimous
upset
usual
utensil
valiant
velocity

vigour
visit
voice
wagging
wanting
war
waste
wheel
whimper
whiskers
whisky
whispered
whist
Whitsuntide
windmill
wise
wives
wolf
wool
working
worrying
worth
wrap
write
writing
wrote
yesterday

Congratulations!

You have now learnt to spell **2,300** words, know what they mean and how to use them in a sentence.

Now move on to **Book 6** to learn lots more words to add to your word bank total.

Answers

Exercise 93a
1) skate
2) safer
3) grief
4) deeper
5) darkness
6) brightest
7) smiling
8) chief
9) hoping
10) hiding

Exercise 93b
11) shining
12) skating
13) brighter
14) finer
15) illness
16) safest
17) cooler
18) thief
19) miner
20) burnt

Crossword No. 93

Letter = N

Exercise 94a
1) Easter
2) poet
3) wrote
4) nearly
5) repeat
6) clay
7) should
8) repair
9) Christmas
10) remove

Exercise 94b
11) poem
12) quickly
13) write
14) prove
15) remark
16) writing
17) cheer
18) wrap
19) grey
20) move

Crossword No. 94

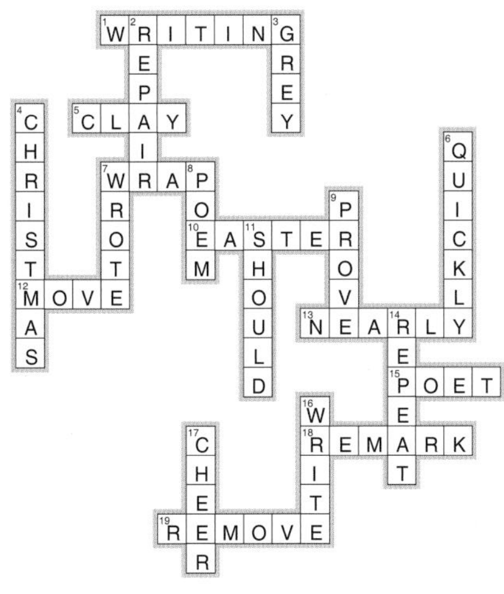

Letter = E

Exercise 95a
1) grandmother
2) breakfast
3) branch
4) yesterday
5) coal
6) peach
7) roast
8) around
9) usual
10) However

Exercise 95b
11) branches
12) afternoon
13) float
14) afraid
15) roam
16) aloud
17) above
18) peaches
19) cloak
20) alike

Crossword No. 95

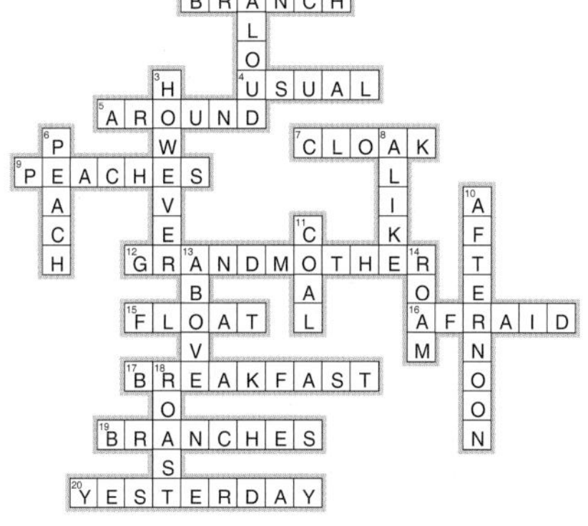

Letter = T

Answers

Exercise 96a

1) stuff
2) glasses
3) husband
4) towards
5) forward
6) border
7) twice
8) fence
9) cuff
10) Copper

Exercise 96b

11) worth
12) together
13) afterwards
14) classes
15) inches
16) pepper
17) starve
18) since
19) order
20) price

Crossword No. 96

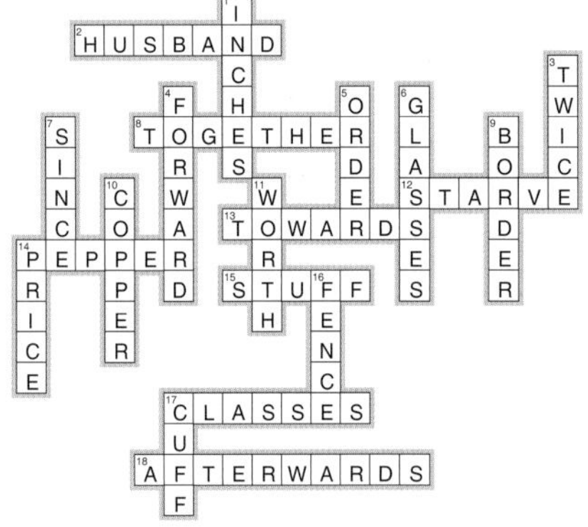

Letter = S

Exercise 97a

1) quiet
2) birth
3) dishes
4) provide
5) track
6) forest
7) friend
8) present
9) bitter
10) fir

Exercise 97b

11) birthday
12) stiff
13) pretend
14) lemon
15) sugar
16) visit
17) boxes
18) dwell
19) silly
20) Hurry

Crossword No. 97

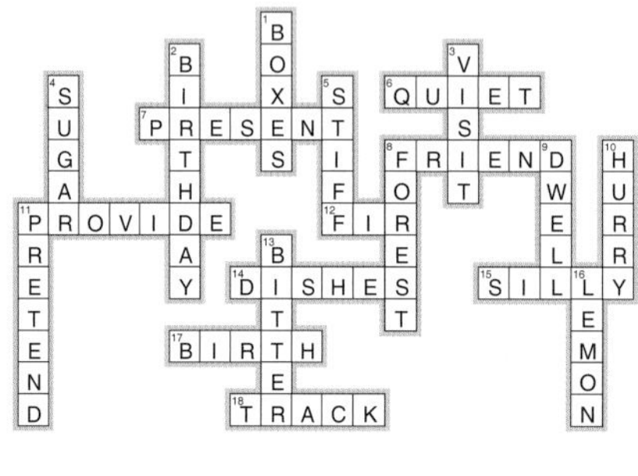

Letter = H

Exercise 98a

1) fourth
2) eleven
3) strip
4) simple
5) wool
6) fifth
7) serve
8) hundred
9) upset
10) tenth

Exercise 98b

11) term
12) cling
13) finger
14) flesh
15) gift
16) pint
17) person
18) four
19) bloom
20) twelve

Crossword No. 98

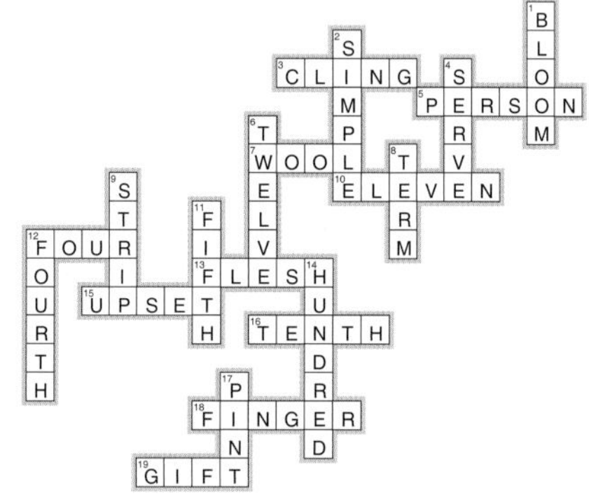

Letter = T

Answers

Exercise 99a
1) steep
2) space
3) soak
4) spider
5) wheel
6) earth
7) lily
8) bravely
9) chance
10) deed

Exercise 99b
11) steel
12) voice
13) earn
14) wise
15) invite
16) soap
17) daisy
18) daisies
19) lilies
20) grace

Crossword No. 99

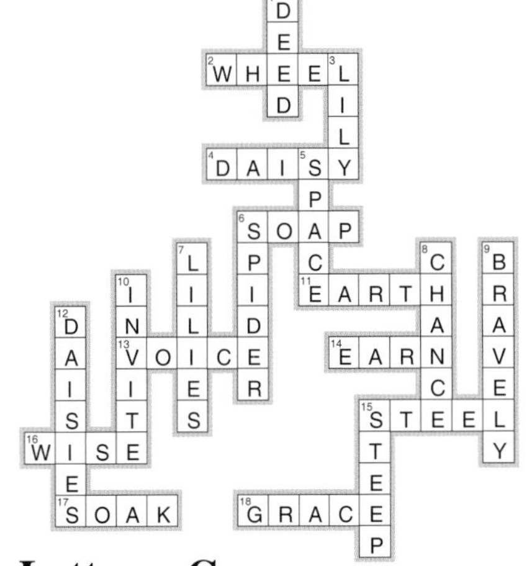

Letter = C

Exercise 100a
1) Thirty
2) twenty
3) thousand
4) loaves
5) between
6) halves
7) thieves
8) fifteen
9) creeping
10) sixty

Exercise 100b
11) thirteen
12) sixteen
13) loaf
14) calf
15) fifty
16) shelf
17) fourteen
18) leaves
19) half
20) indeed

Crossword No. 100

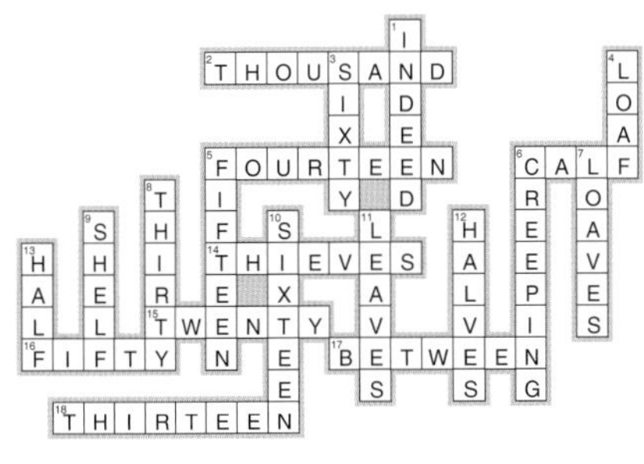

Letter = U

Exercise 101a
1) knot
2) themselves
3) fixed
4) flew
5) thrown
6) knives
7) crew
8) chew
9) wolf
10) jail

Exercise 101b
11) snail
12) wives
13) mail
14) knock
15) kneel
16) knee
17) threw
18) rail
19) knife
20) grind

Crossword No. 101

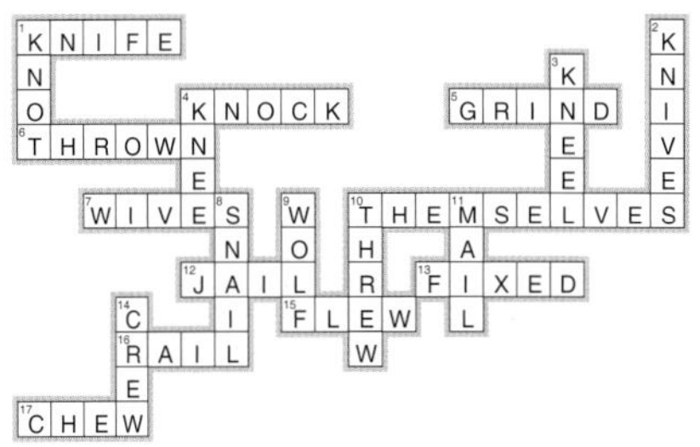

Letter = I

In the Living Room

1. VASE
2. BOOKCASE
3. PEN
4. MAGAZINE
5. HEARTH
6. PLANT
7. SETTEE
8. CUSHION
9. SPEAKER
10. NEWSPAPER
11. PLUG
12. TELEVISION
13. MANTELPIECE
14. CANDLE
15. ARMCHAIR

In the Bathroom

1. TOILET
2. WATER
3. SOAP
4. SHOWER GEL
5. SHOWER
6. PEDESTAL
7. TOOTHBRUSH
8. WASH BASIN
9. MAT
10. TOOTHPASTE
11. TOWEL
12. RAZOR
13. CISTERN
14. TAPS
15. SCALES

Answers

Exercise 102a
1) dying
2) strike
3) picture
4) deaf
5) raise
6) finish
7) paid
8) sure
9) raised
10) cure

Exercise 102b
11) heaven
12) capture
13) trunk
14) dread
15) lying
16) flock
17) tie
18) pure
19) defend
20) tied

Crossword No. 102

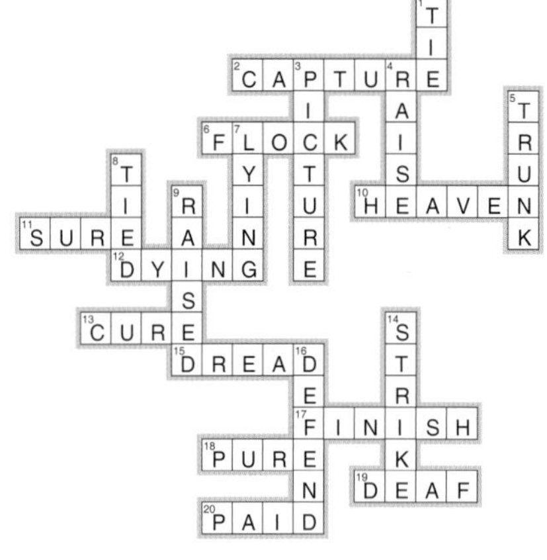

Letter = C

Exercise 103a
1) kettle
2) swimming
3) battle
4) rate
5) manner
6) rattle
7) built
8) frame
9) matter
10) cattle

Exercise 103b
11) scrape
12) bottle
13) building
14) content
15) slipped
16) sore
17) flame
18) cork
19) tired
20) build

Crossword No. 103

Letter = T

Exercise 104a
1) easier
2) butterflies
3) heavy
4) trying
5) shy
6) axe
7) easiest
8) flying
9) heaviest
10) spy

Exercise 104b
11) heavier
12) rank
13) toe
14) shout
15) merrily
16) War
17) easily
18) army
19) Scout
20) answer

Crossword No. 104

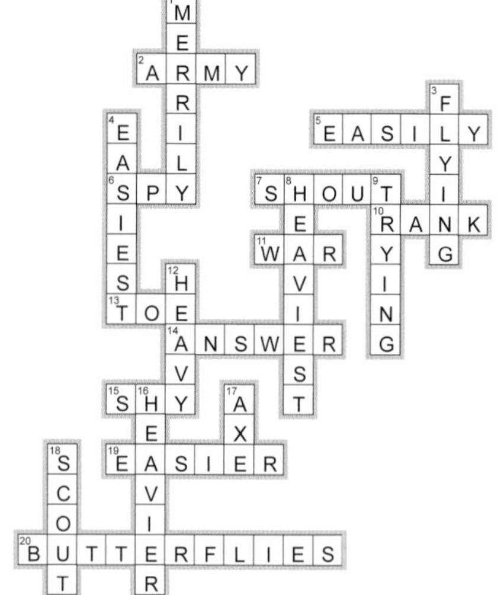

Letter = R

Answers

Exercise 105a

1) mast
2) instant
3) goodbye
4) copy
5) fasten
6) starch
7) taste
8) arch
9) because
10) haste

Exercise 105b

11) shadow
12) empty
13) being
14) pity
15) plenty
16) touch
17) waste
18) cause
19) past
20) odd

Crossword No. 105

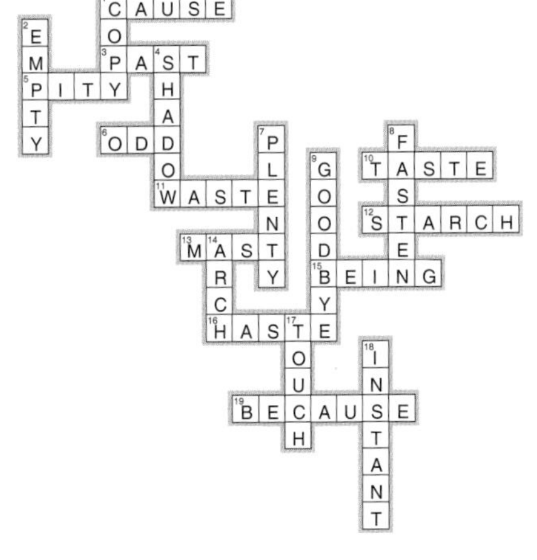

Letter = P

Exercise 106a

1) postage
2) Forty
3) glory
4) remind
5) export
6) import
7) manage
8) police
9) loss
10) savage

Exercise 106b

11) repent
12) respond
13) notice
14) slice
15) package
16) lose
17) report
18) record
19) splice
20) history

Crossword No. 106

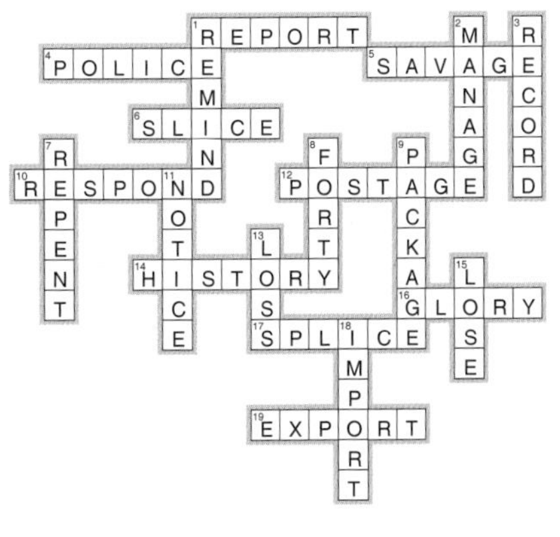

Letter = O

Exercise 107a

1) rheumatism
2) monastery
3) pylon
4) rhubarb
5) confectioner
6) ironmonger
7) journalist
8) marquee
9) windmill
10) Dome

Exercise 107b

11) bungalow
12) fruitier
13) hangar
14) jeweller
15) accordion
16) secretary
17) tobacconist
18) detective
19) buccaneer
20) stationer

Crossword No. 107

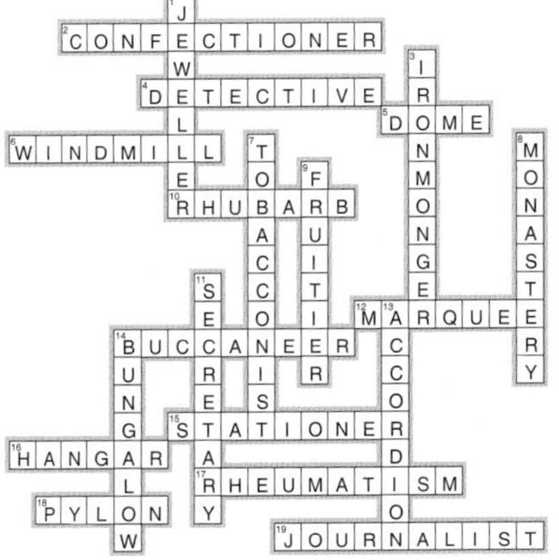

Letter = A

At the Dentist

1. JACKET 2. INSTRUMENTS 3. TISSUES 4. TUNIC 5. X-RAY
6. COMPUTER 7. TOOTH 8. SYRINGE 9. GLOVES 10. POSTER
11. DENTAL NURSE 12. CHAIR 13. MOUTHWASH 14. BASIN 15. DENTURES

In the Accident & Emergency Department

1. STETHOSCOPE 2. AMBULANCE 3. PATIENT 4. PILLS 5. MONITOR
6. CHART 7. SEAT 8. DOCTOR 9. CURTAIN 10. CYLINDER
11. BLANKET 12. BANDAGE 13. TROLLEY 14. FORM 15. MATTRESS

Answers

Exercise 108a

1) granary
2) eighty
3) Whitsuntide
4) conceited
5) announcer
6) receipt
7) whist
8) velocity
9) abattoir
10) whisky

Exercise 108b

11) restaurant
12) democracy
13) cannibal
14) novelty
15) whispered
16) honesty
17) penniless
18) whiskers
19) whimper
20) detergent

Crossword No. 108

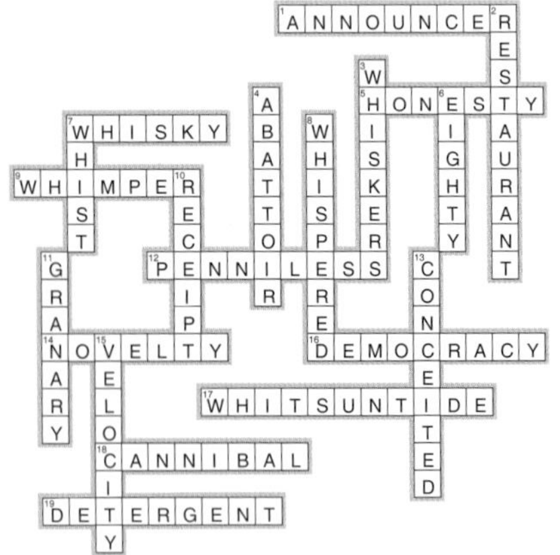

Letter = I

Exercise 109a

1) hare
2) diagonal
3) toboggan
4) motorcycle
5) daffodil
6) boulder
7) peregrine
8) utensil
9) foliage
10) smoulder

Exercise 109b

11) tonsil
12) luggage
13) rocket
14) leggings
15) maggot
16) athlete
17) stencil
18) begging
19) lentil
20) clipper

Crossword No. 109

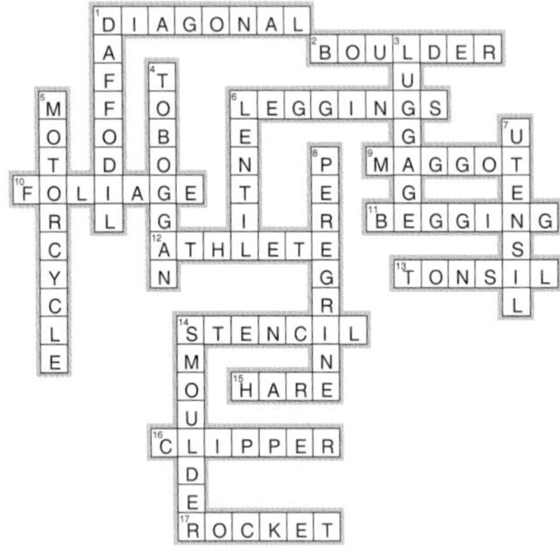

Letter = A

Exercise 110a

1) miraculous
2) hose
3) miscellaneous
4) ambulance
5) firemen
6) civilians
7) valiant
8) casualty
9) satisfied
10) diameter

Exercise 110b

11) defied
12) monotonous
13) magnified
14) dignified
15) humorous
16) unanimous
17) hideous
18) financial
19) tense
20) crucified

Crossword No. 110

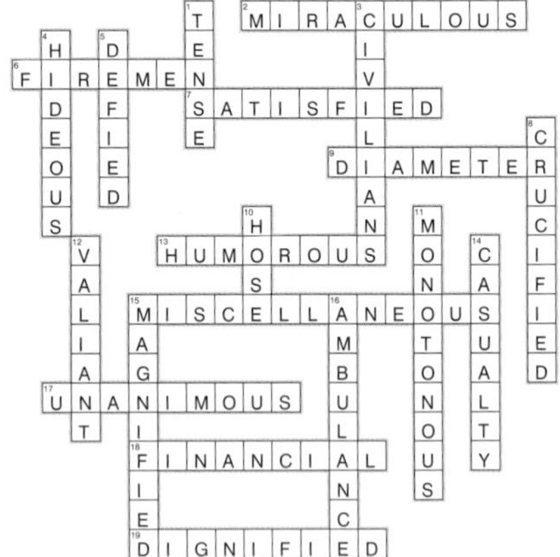

Letter = F

Answers

Exercise 111a
1) anonymous
2) armoured
3) painful
4) colourful
5) contour
6) beautifully
7) vigour
8) forecast
9) dreadful
10) foreman

Exercise 111b
11) lawfully
12) dolefully
13) splendour
14) cheerfully
15) foremost
16) merciful
17) forearm
18) tasteful
19) painfully
20) truthfully

Crossword No. 111

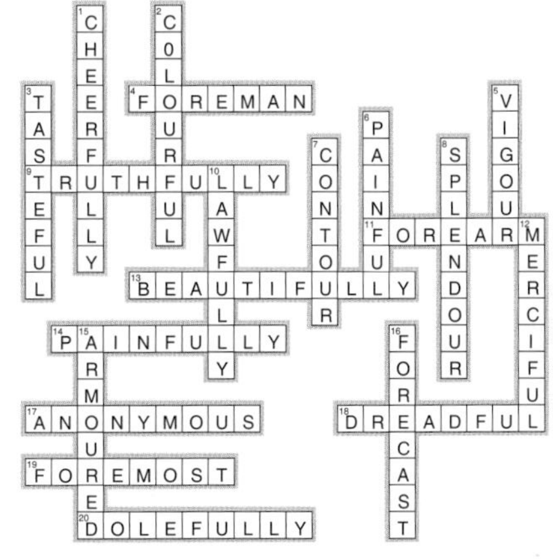

Letter = R

Exercise 112a
1) drizzle
2) apprentice
3) excel
4) ketchup
5) apparatus
6) bullying
7) burying
8) flask
9) hurrying
10) copying

Exercise 112b
11) appalling
12) scowl
13) flop
14) replying
15) appetite
16) sway
17) denying
18) worrying
19) pitying
20) baffle

Crossword No. 112

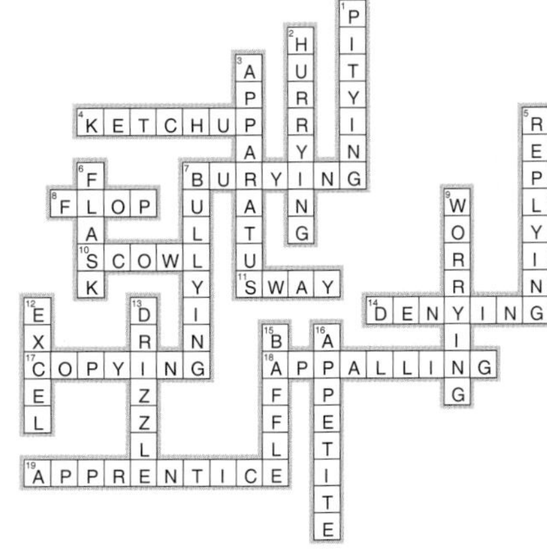

Letter = P

Exercise 113a
1) muzzle
2) oxygen
3) twinkle
4) scrabble
5) scotch
6) bleach
7) fizz
8) quintuplets
9) crutches
10) planet

Exercise 113b
11) squaw
12) jogging
13) cider
14) stray
15) blink
16) drowsy
17) huge
18) wagging
19) pounce
20) droop

Crossword No. 113

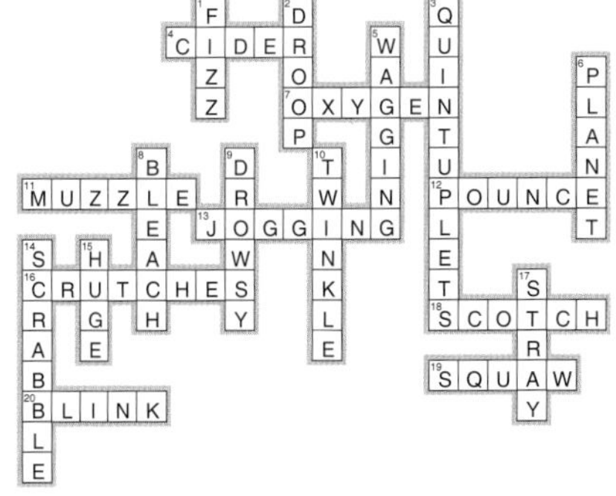

Letter = N

Answers

Exercise 114a
1) bruising
2) dandruff
3) catches
4) tandoori
5) paperback
6) florist
7) plaice
8) scooter
9) multiplication
10) sizzle

Exercise 114b
11) scab
12) fattest
13) batch
14) twist
15) screech
16) bigger
17) stride
18) hiss
19) amount
20) step

Crossword No. 114

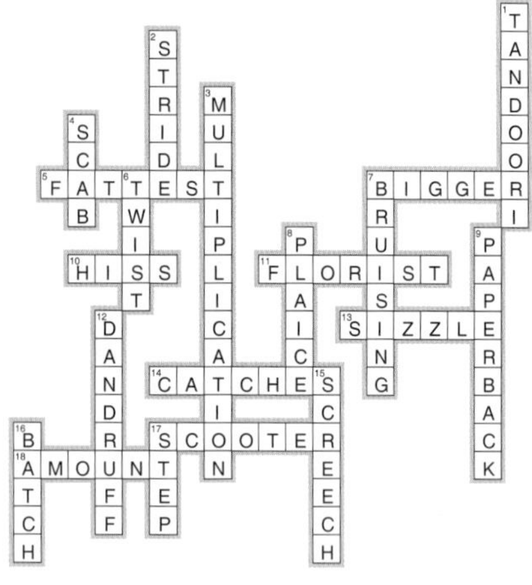

Letter = F

Exercise 115a
1) working
2) cruising
3) taller
4) pawn
5) ditches
6) Attorney
7) comment
8) cleanest
9) wanting
10) circled

Exercise 115b
11) sunshine
12) emphasis
13) saddest
14) suitor
15) thirst
16) darker
17) counts
18) sharpest
19) thatched
20) qualify

Crossword No. 115

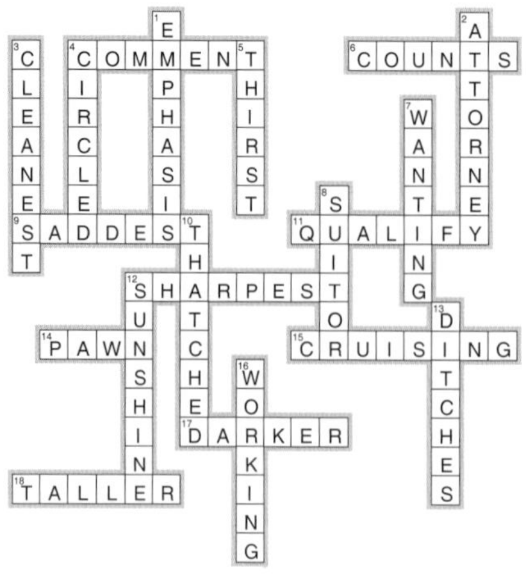

Letter = A

PROGRESS CHARTS

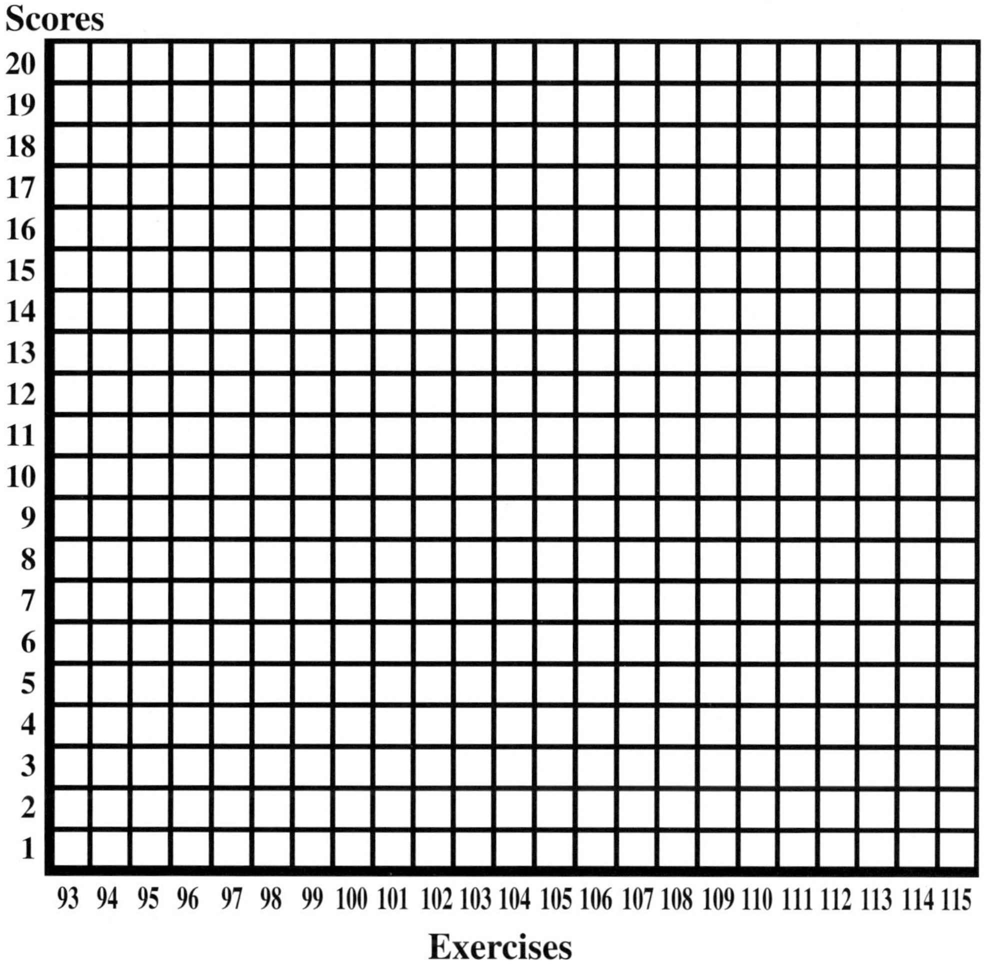

Scores
20 19 18 17 16 15 14 13 12 11 10 9 8 7 6 5 4 3 2 1
93 94 95 96 97 98 99 100 101 102 103 104 105 106 107 108 109 110 111 112 113 114 115
Exercises

Shade in your score for each exercise on the graph. Add them up for your total score out of 460. Ask an adult to work out the percentage.

Total Score

Percentage

% **A**

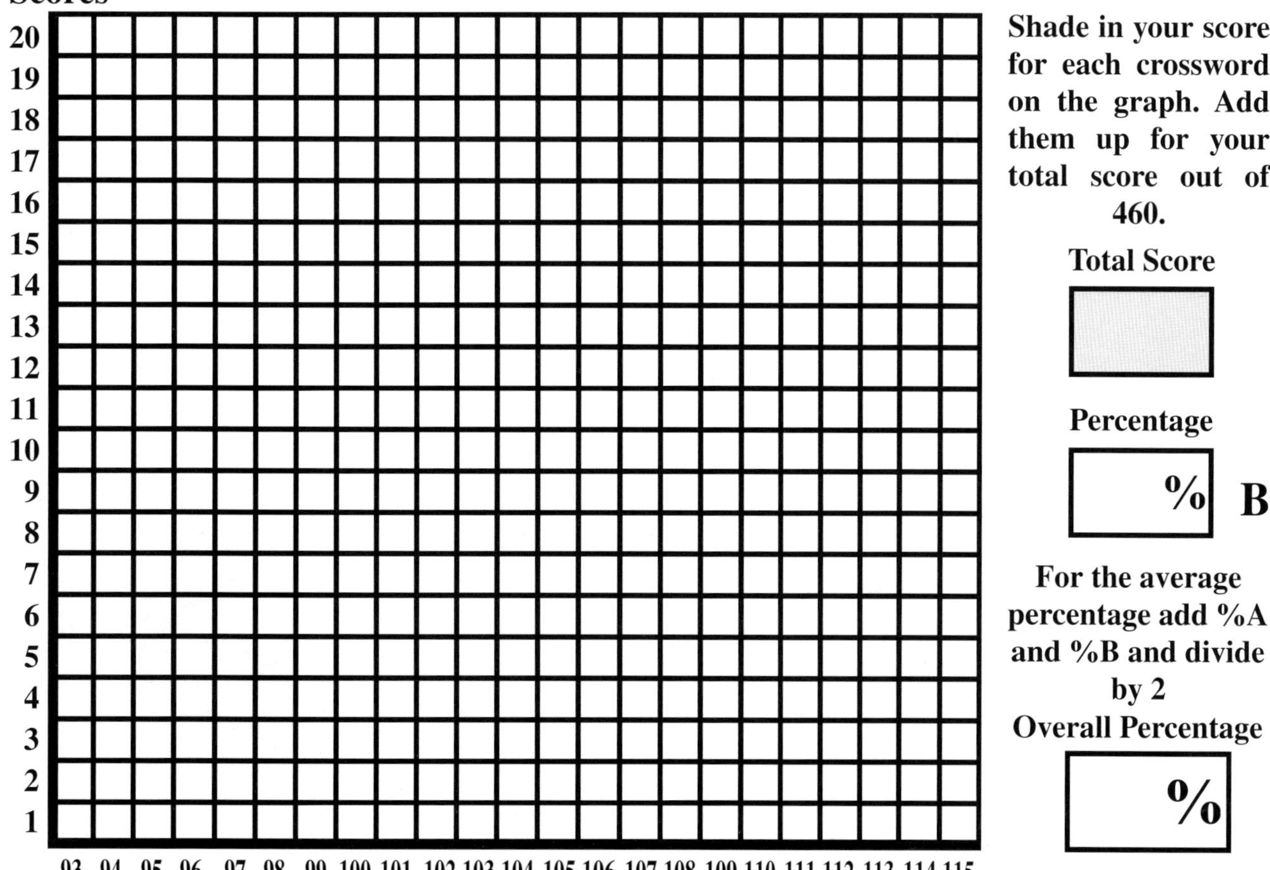

Scores
20 19 18 17 16 15 14 13 12 11 10 9 8 7 6 5 4 3 2 1
93 94 95 96 97 98 99 100 101 102 103 104 105 106 107 108 109 110 111 112 113 114 115
Crosswords

Shade in your score for each crossword on the graph. Add them up for your total score out of 460.

Total Score

Percentage

% **B**

For the average percentage add %A and %B and divide by 2

Overall Percentage

%

CERTIFICATE OF

ACHIEVEMENT

This certifies

____

has successfully completed

Key Stage 2

Spelling & Vocabulary

WORKBOOK **5**

Overall percentage score achieved [ ] %

Comment ____________________________________

____

Signed ____________________________________
(teacher/parent/guardian)

Date ____________________________________